The Power of Silence

by

Horatio W. Dresser

Chapter I
The Point of View

—

NOW that the nineteenth century has ended and scholars are making their estimates of its many tendencies, it is becoming more and more clear that it is to be known as the century of the philosophy of evolution. It has been an eminently practical era, the age of mechanical invention and discovery, and, toward its close, an epoch of sociological inquiry. But the philosophy of evolution came first, and the unprecedented inquiry into causes, sources, origins, prepared the way for the profound interests which marked the transition to the present century. No department of thought has escaped this reconstructive spirit. It is today a truism to declare that no event or person can be understood apart from environment and from evolutionary history.

Sometimes the inroads of science have seemed to threaten the foundations of man's most sacred faith. But in the end the essentials of faith have been marvellously enriched. The widespread inquiry into customs, traditions, races, and religions has tended toward the unification of all our thinking about mankind. Hence, many distinctions between creeds and doctrines have faded out in the light of the larger sympathy and sense of brotherhood which the inquiry has inspired. A new spirit of tolerance has brought a willingness to admit that, despite all differences in creed and dogma, men who are really in earnest are striving for the same great ends, the world over. The important consideration is to know how far a man has advanced in moral and religious evolution, what manner of life he lives.

This new demand that man shall understand himself in the light of all the causes that have operated to produce him has still more significance when we turn from the outer world to the inner. Thus far, evolutionary science has dealt with man in large part as a physical being. There was a time, in fact, during the middle of the nineteenth century when the entire inquiry seemed to make for materialism. Closer scrutiny of the results showed, however, that the ultimate problems of life, the questions concerning the real nature of existence, the character of the real man, and the like, were left for idealistic philosophy to solve. We now know that to maintain the evolutionary point of view is by no means to be materialistic. At any rate, evolutionary materialism is a failure. There are decided limits beyond which mere evolutionism has been unable to go. It is difficult also for natural science to advance into the inner world, for science deals with the universal, and the inner life is in a peculiar sense the home of the individual. Even experimental psychology fails in the attempt to discover the true character of the inner life. The most interesting questions are still unanswered when psychology has completed its description of our states of consciousness. In fact psychology as a natural science explicitly disclaims the right to ascertain the values of inner experience or discover the nature of the self. It is necessary, if the search for origins is to be complete, for each man to take up the work where science leaves it, and pursue the investigation by the same fruitful method of systematic research.

There are plenty of sceptics to raise objections to any such procedure. It will be said that the era of morbid self-examination and conscientiousness will again return. Others will insist that the inner life is a mystery past finding out. To all this the reply is that man already lives in and knows much about the inner life. This is no new venture. It is only a question of substituting more knowledge for less knowledge. It is the half-way positions of imprisoning self-consciousness that distress us. There is no inherent danger in analytical self-knowledge or rational synthesis. The essential is that such analysis and synthesis shall be thorough. Ordinarily out self-knowledge stops short of the most important consideration. If we are to be thorough, we must ask, What is man's ultimate origin? What is his real environment? Whither is he tending? These are profound philosophical questions, to be sure. But there are respects in which they are also problems for experimental investigation. No man is more truly a child of this practical age than the one who approaches these issues in the spirit of empirical research.

Individual man now has far more material to draw upon in his effort to investigate the inner life in a free, profitable spirit. Whatever one may think of the conclusions which bear upon the belief in a future life, it is clear that the finer aspects of psychic research have thrown light upon the mysteries of the inner world. Meanwhile, a new science has been springing up, midway between experimental psychology and the realm of the individual soul, namely, the psychology of religion; and a new literature of the soul has also begun to appear. It remains for the individual to seize upon the results of all this finer, more exact thinking, and verify or correct them in the light of personal problems. The farther science advances into the inner world the easier it will be to avoid imprisoning subjectivism.

The essential is to approach the study in the right temper. In a sense the inner life is a gift which all men share. Its universal characteristics each man may verify. What makes it real is the fact that each of us just now possesses it. First of all it is owned and observed as experience. It pulsates, presents new moments even while we observe it. Every man is in possession of clues which will reveal the deeper meanings of this surging stream. For every man has perplexities which have been postponed and postponed, not because they are insoluble but simply because these difficulties have not been met in precisely the situation where they arose. It seems probable that the interest, the problem of the living present is the most direct clue to the larger truth of life as a whole. Hence it is perspective that we need, not the limited point of view of morbid introspection. We must regard our own little moment of life in the same comprehensive spirit wherewith the geologist approaches the phenomena of an epoch in the earth's history. We should view life as a whole, as a tendency amidst a universal environment. In short, we must begin at last to be philosophical.

To begin to be philosophical is to be thorough, moderate, painstaking; to pursue truth wherever it may lead. The venture seems too bold, at first thought. But again it is profoundly simple, since it is concerned with the commonest experiences of life and in a particular sense with the individual interest of the observer. It is clear that life is a problem which has for each an individual solution. No one can wholly solve it for us, precisely because it possesses this individual element. Life has had its particular history in each case. In every instance it wears a different aspect. The temperamental distinction which once seemed baffling therefore proves to be the clue to intelligent thinking.

The utmost that one individual may do for an other is to state the facts and laws of life as he apprehends them. That is, another may present the universal element; it is the particular application which makes it true. Hence each man must investigate for himself. Hence each man must think. And thinking is not so hard a task after all. We make it difficult because we think in borrowed terms, or because we have no method.

The present volume is primarily intended to further the kind of inquiry here outlined. The references to the present age and to current literature suggest the possibility of taking a still more practical step. Where all this literature ends as science, the art of the inner life begins for the individual. In the present teaching no mere acceptance of belief is called for. No dogma is here insisted upon. No claim is made either for originality or finality. The essential is actual study of life at first hand. Hence, one should be free to depart from prepossessions; not that the creeds of the past are untrue, but that one is just now searching into the realities which give rise to creeds, one is endeavouring to know life itself. For the main trouble with us is, perhaps, that we adopt the opinions of others about life; we read and read and read; we hear and we hear and we listen. Meanwhile, the great thing is not the words but the spirit, the meaning. The spirit each man of us has with him. No fact of life is more important than this present instant. Nowhere in all the universe is more truth compacted than into this living reality—the passing stream of consciousness which links us to the world, to past and future, heaven and the Father of all.

It is essential, then, that at each point in the discussion the reader pause to make the thought his own through quiet realisation of its spirit and its meaning. Let him pause to ask, What does this mean for me? How does it explain, how does it accord or conflict with my experience? Have I ever devoted time and reflection—alone with my deeper self—to realise the full bearing of the profoundest and sublimest truths of life? Have I ever made them my own and actualised them in daily life, or is there still a chasm between theory and practice?

If the reader will keep this practical object constantly in view, unsuspected applications of well-known truths will become apparent before he finishes the volume.

If one is to pass beyond mere self-analysis of the usual sort it is clear, however, that one must be willing to entertain the thought of a fundamental system of realities. To end in a large world one must begin with broad premises. If man's life is environed by a larger Life, he cannot understand himself alone. In deepest truth there is no "alone." Our own experimental observation proves that, first of all. It seems impossible even to outline one's method of investigation without admitting that the presence of an environing Life is the most striking consideration.

What that Life shall be called is of course another question. But for one's self the frank admission must be made at the outset that it is the presence of the divine Father, without whom the most elementary fact seems unintelligible. If the reader names it otherwise—well and good. It is not now a question of names. As a possible aid to inquiry, the present discussion is confessedly a chapter from life, an appeal to life. The aim is to convey the living reality itself; so far as possible, instead of merely talking about it. Hence the appeal is to the profoundest experience of the reader—recognised, confessed as what it most genuinely reveals itself to be. The appeal is to reason, too. But reason must start with facts, with actual life; it does not create its own objects. How else can one hope to unite philosophy and life than by this frank union of experience and thought—one's deepest life made explicit?

It is obviously wiser to be true to all aspects of life as it appears from the angle of one's own temperament and experience than to force all facts into a certain system. The deepest facts are usually slighted, if not excluded, by the latter process. No formula seems large enough to cover all we know and feel. There is an element in experience that usually eludes description. Some experiences can never be told. They are intimately a part of us. They are sacred, and one hesitates to speak of them. Yet one can suggest them, or at least let it be known that in these rarest moments of existence one seemed most truly to live; Only in this way does the soul, that part of us which is most truly individual, find expression. Only in this way does the unfettered soul show its freedom from prejudice and dogma. Allegiance to a person or theory limits one to the particular view of life represented by that person or theory. To claim finality for one's system would be equivalent to affirming that progress shall end with the particular discussion in question. Our theories serve us well while we remember that life itself is larger.

Life, then, is large, let us say once for all, and demands a broad way of thinking about it. Ordinarily, we have no sense of what our total self means, We suffer, and we seek relief. We are absorbed in the present, in its needs and woes, unaware that our whole past lives, our inheritance, and our temperament, may affect this bit of suffering nature which for the moment limits our thought. We live as though time were soon to cease, and prudence would not permit us an hour for quiet reflection.

Yet a new phase, and to some the happiest phase, of life begins when they stop hurried thought, and try quietly to realise what life means as an advancing whole. If life is in some sense one system, can any other interpretation be rational, will the parts ever assume their true relationship in our minds except when viewed in the light of the whole? Possibly our suffering is largely unnecessary. Possibly it has come about because we have failed to adjust our thought to the wholeness of things. At any rate, to take time, at last, to isolate one's self from the rushing tide of daily life and to raise the great questions here proposed, is to begin in earnest to experiment.

From the first, one stands in need of all sorts of conclusions which seem to belong rather to the end. It is one thing to talk about "the power of silence" and another to be able to pause long enough to enjoy it. One is eager to know what that power is. Yet one must first have a basis to stand upon. The fact that a relatively obscure element besets all our thinking about the inner life is no excuse for vagueness. To fall back upon feeling or faith alone will no longer suffice. We are in quest of the whole, and reason is surely a part of life's whole. There is both the hurrying flux of our tantalising consciousness, the part of life which refuses to be still; and there is the persistent conviction that life has a deeper reality which it is the office of calmer thinking to discover. Clearly, we must take life as we find it, and move forward, faithful alike to feeling and to thought.

One fact, however, is clear: experience is best explained at the outset by reference to its environment. If the problem seems too large for us, at first, it would surely prove more difficult if we tried to leap beyond present experience. It is only a question of attaining closer and closer acquaintance with the near at hand. If our logic at last compels us to look beyond immediate experience in search of its basis, then that basis must be such as actual life demands.

The truth is involved in the very nature of the beings and things by which we are surrounded. It only needs to be evolved or made explicit. All power is immanent, it works through something. Man should not look beyond his own nature, his temperament, inheritance, education, until he is compelled to do so in order to find an adequate explanation of his experience. He should have a clear conception of the closely related events out of which his life has proceeded, as the river is enlarged and shaped in its course by its tributaries and the country through which it flows, yet never rises higher than its source. In a word, he must know his origin, both immediate and remote. He must start with personal experience, but should not stop until he has traced it to the Source beyond which thought cannot go.

The point of view of this book, then, is explicitly empirical. By the term "empirical" as here used is meant that our existence in the universe is made known through experience, and that by studying experience, testing our theories by further experience, and keeping close to the assured results, we may not only solve our practical problems but gain knowledge of life as a whole. That is to say, experience brings changes. We reflect upon those changes and experiment. By experiment we learn what theories are sound and piactical, what are absurd. The purpose of out theories is to explain experience, and further experience, rationally tested, shows whether or not we have succeeded. Each of us possesses experience and each man may experiment for himself. Experience means much or little according to the degree of individual experiment. To gain more knowledge of the sort that is really worthwhile a man must put more theories to the test, observe more acutely, think more seriously.

It may well be that experience as individually made known to us is unable fully to account for itself. Something more than mere description is called for. The question, What is the nature of experience? leads directly to idealistic analysis and ultimately to some sort of constructive idealism, that is, a systematic restatement of the data of experience in terms of reason. But we are not here concerned with the ultimate unification of the data of experience. Nor are we concerned with the more theoretical evidences for idealism. To be sure, we must introduce certain arguments, for example, a plea for the immanence of God. But the chief value of these arguments will be found in their practical empirical bearings. That is, the argument for the divine immanence, or for the idealistic interpretation of experience, will serve as a central line of thought by the pursuit of which the reader may follow the developments of his own experience. In other words, it is the value or meaning which the reader attributes to the argument that is of consequence. The first-hand evidence is of more import than the theoretical description. But once in fuller possession of the empirical evidence, one is in a position to follow the philosophical implications much further than the present arguments carry them.

Three important distinctions are involved in this brief outline. (1) First there is the question of fact. For example, there is experience of a religious type, an emotional uplift or sense of worship. (2) There is the particular theory brought forward to account for the fact. If you are a pantheist, you will conclude that in the ineffable religious moment you are identical with the "Absolute." But if you are a theist, you will revere God as the Father and indulge in no mystical theories of identification. (3) Further more there are the practical values which you attach to the facts. If you conclude that God is the Father, your conduct will differ greatly from that of the mystic. In the end, it is undoubtedly the values which we attribute to experience that influence us most. For values are ideals, and we develop by means of ideals. Ordinarily it is only the technical philosopher who distinguishes thus sharply between facts, theories, and values. But the distinction is plainly of great importance. Very few people know what a fact is. The majority read their opinions into the given matters of experience and mistake what they want to believe for what is so. But one can make little headway in the endeavour to understand experience without constant discrimination between fact and theory. And there is clearly a great difference between that which is and that which may, or ought to be.

The present inquiry will be chiefly based on these distinctions. The reader is already in possesion of facts, that is, of experience. He also possesses abundant theories. Modern science describes for him the physical world in which he lives. History narrates man's life in the past. Moral science sets forth the views of men in regard to what ought to be. Christianity is an inculcation of religious principles. Philosophy is the intelligent co-ordination of all theories. But there is need of an art of life which shall show man how to live philosophically. This, the most practical of arts, each man may contribute to by giving thought to the problems and laws of his own experience. What he most needs is a working ideal, a principle by which to apply philosophy more successfully. Hence the importance of ideals, the realisational aspect of religious teaching, the practical worth of philosophical thinking. Hence, too, the value of silence, of sufficient repose to enable a man to realise the meaning, the spirit of what he believes.

For this inquiry the reader needs no other equipment than he already possesses. Each of us is feeling, acting, living amidst the great stream of events which we call "experience." Yonder are the fields and the hills. Above is the fair, blue sky. Near at hand are the houses of friends and neighbours—theatres of fascinating interests. Within the mind there are passing thoughts and varying emotions. Implied in all these transient mental states are the habits by which we have developed, and the convictions which underlie our conduct. The essential is to awaken to consciousness of this surging play of circumstance, discover how we are taking it, and consider how we may become more wisely adjusted. This is to enter more fully into the spirit of the age, to become philosophers of evolution in a yet profounder sense. For it shows not only how experience leads to experience, but even how thought follows thought. Thus we may enter into the fulness of life as it passes, and by this profounder mastery win the greater repose. And he who can break away from the age sufficiently to meditate upon it in peace is indeed ready to apprehend its finest values, to live in it yet not of it.

Chapter II
The Immanent God

—

IT is characteristic of empiricists to make as few assumptions as possible, to plunge into life and begin to philosophise. All that need be said at the outset is that one finds one's self existing in the world, with a deep desire to understand the nature and meaning of life. Where the world came from, one cannot now say. The important consideration is that it somehow came, and with it this strange being called one's "self." If we do not yet see the rationale of it, we at any rate possess the wonderful gift known as "experience."

Wherever we begin to rationalise, we shall come out at the same point, and ask the same questions, if we persist until we discover ultimate principles. It is usual to begin an inquiry into the nature of experience by analysing the presentations of consciousness. But as we are in the first place interested to apply the empirical method, it is desirable to begin with a well-known argument and note the changes which practical empiricism brings about in all our thinking. In no respect has the critical empirical method wrought a greater change than in regard to the argument for the existence of God. Hence it is the understanding of the change thus wrought that most readily prepares the way for what is to follow.

It has long been customary, for example, to support the argument for God's existence by an appeal to the sequence of certain causal phenomena. From the fact of causation in general it seems to be an easy step to the proof that God is the "first cause." For example, it is plain that when a message is flashed over the wires from town to town, or when the electric car transports us through the city streets, an efficient cause has produced the effect which serves us so readily. The rapidity with which the effect results does not deceive us. We may know little about the force in question; but we know that it acts in unvarying accordance with certain laws, the understanding of which enables us to control it. We learn further that every cause has its antecedent. The electricity is generated by the aid of energy derived primarily from the sun. The motion of the ship, as it sails before the wind, is likewise traceable from wind to sun, from the sun to the primal source of motion in the universe at large. And we stop here only because we know not the antecedent of this first activity.

The chain of causes and effects is in reality endless. Without a cause nothing can happen, nothing could ever have happened; and with eternally active causes in the world something must always happen. Every cause, every effect, every event in the history of the universe and in our own physical existence, is inseparably connected with this infinite series, extending far back into the irrevocable past, and potentially related to an ever-dawning future.

Yet, if we ask, What does this endless causal series signify? When did cause and effect begin? it is clear that the mere possession of such a series is of slight consequence. For there is no point at which thought can stop and declare, This cause is final; before its appearance there was no activity. A merely temporal beginning of events is unintelligible. The utmost that one can allege is that there must be one all-embracing series of causes and effects which has existed eternally, a series of which our world is a part and of which all future activity will be an outgrowth. Yet, if the temporal chain of causes and effects must have a ground other than itself, if God could not have been a merely temporal creator, we must look beyond causation altogether to find the true reality of things.

In order to test this reasoning, try for a moment to conceive of the universe as an absolute void, then imagine the creation of something or of some being in this mere emptiness. Such an event is utterly inconceivable, since something could not be a product of nothing, and every result must have an efficient and substantial basis. If, then, something can neither be made from nothing, nor something become non-existent, the sum total of substance would seem to be ultimately the same. It can be modified, evolved, or dissolved, but must itself have an eternal basis.

Try now to imagine a condition of things in which there should be no motion, and conceive the beginning of motion in the illimitable and perfectly inert universe which you have conjured from the fanciful deep. Once more the attempt is futile. Absolute and universal rest, like a perfect void, is inconceivable. Something moving would be needed wherewith to start motion, as something substantial must have existed before a new product could result. If only one particle moved, then something moving must have caused its motion; and, if it moved once only, all existing particles would undoubtedly be set in motion in the course of time. Motion could not cease, since only a moving power could stop it, and there would be no power to stop this inhibiting force.

The cessation of motion, then, like its inception, is unthinkable. If it were not continuous, eternal, it apparently could never have become a fact. Moreover, motion implies not only a continuous, all-embracing series of causes and effects, but the existence of the eternally moving substance already postulated. Physical motion also means change from place to place, from one condition to another. Change in turn implies the experience of rhythm or interval in motion. Change also implies the existence of space, or the extension in three directions of that which is moved.

Thus an eternally existing substance, uncreated and never-ceasing motion, and infinite space, seem to be inseparably connected. There is cause and effect, duration between them, extension of that which is moved or affected, eternal motion, and an ever-moving something whose activity is thus characterised.

That is to say, all that is gained by this kind of reasoning is the mere pursuit of one fact to another, one principle to another. All that we have as a result is a collection of considerations which give promise of ultimate truth but never lead beyond this elusive pursuit. What we need is not a "cause" of all things, not a continuously moving "substance," but an eternal Ground or Reality. This Ground is as readily discoverable here and now, as at any moment, in any age or time. For, as it is the Ground of all existence, it is itself beyond all causality; it never came to be, nor will it ever cease to exist; it simply is. It is not mere "cause," but the ultimate source alike of the substance and the power exhibited in what we denominate "causality." It is that Being wherewith all thought pauses when, having given up the pursuit of temporal sequences, the mind turns at last from abstract argument to acknowledge the living, present God.

Hence God as the ultimate Ground of the universe is the Being who needs no further explanation. He is self-existent, uncreated, indestructible, at once the basis and the life of all that is known in the universe of change. He is simply the supreme Reality, that for which we need seek no proof, since we are compelled to assume it in the reasoning whereby we hope to prove its existence. The supreme Reality eternally is its own reason for being. It is the ultimate source of consciousness and thought, the final ground of reason. It is the unseen and permanent Life of the visible and transient series of causes and effects which constitute world-experience. It is the Supreme Spirit, the All-Father. Hence the knowledge of the existence of this eternal Reality is the surest possession of human reason.*

There is, of course, a difference between the conception of reality as ultimate Ground, and the religious belief in a personal God.

Were we to conceive of the existence of a vast number of causes in place of the supreme Reality, these causes would be in some sense related, and we should then have need of an eternal ground of this relationship. If there were other realities, those realities would still belong to an ultimate system. There could be but one strictly ultimate, eternal, omnipresent, independent or self-existent reality. However we approach the subject, we are driven to the same end. Thought must stop somewhere. All our endeavours to conceive of the ultimate nature of things lead in time to the conclusion that there is a system which includes all particular starting-points, is in some sense superior to time and place, but is no less truly needed everywhere, in all time and by all thought.

To arrive at this conclusion is to cease to be troubled when one tries to find God by tracing back an infinite series of causes. What is really meant by the term "infinite" is the vague, the indefinite, that which gives thought its pause. In vain do we look for the Father by putting Him thus far from us. It is no wonder that we cannot realise what we mean when we thus describe God negatively. On the other hand, the way to the Father is plain and direct, if we seek Him in the living realities of today.

It is still difficult, to be sure, to define the eternal Reality in an ultimate sense. Yet each definition expresses a truth or attribute. If to define is to limit, nevertheless all definitions that embody the supreme facts and values of life have a common sound in the divine nature. When we state, for example, that "God is love," we truly express a specific characteristic of the most ultimate, eternal, omnipresent Reality. Again, when we speak of the divine wisdom we name a true attribute of the very Mind which has so often and so unjustly been called "inscrutable."

Could we know the Father in all His fulness of wisdom and love we would no doubt be the Father. Could we adequately state His purpose, we should be in full possession of the wondrous beauty of the universe of manifestation. When we apply particular terms to the divine Life and Beauty, we are not defining the universal effulgence, but rather a certain manifestation as it appeals to finite experience. When we declare that we know Him, meaning a personal God, we confess the limitations of our thought. But to argue from this that we do not, or cannot know God at all is entirely unwarranted. It is not God in general whom we really seek to know, but the ever-present Father whom the heart calls "love" and the mind calls "wisdom," the God who is not less but more than these human expressions signify.

It might seem more rational to conceive of God and the universe as "in the making." This would appear to be a logical carrying out of the theory of evolution. But here, again, there is need of a permanent principle, something more than the merely temporal flux of events. Moreover, there is far too much evidence that the universe possesses a definite character, already deeply established, to permit one to accept such a view. It is the need that is felt for a permanent ground of all transient phenomena which leads men to conceive of God as eternal and immutable. To conceive of God as more real than the fluctuations of the time-world is to see that He is more than the world of His manifestation. All our conceptions prove inadequate if they stop short of the eternal. All our conceptions fail if we regard the Father merely from the point of view of our own sonship. Hence there is need of both the philosophical conception of reality as ultimate Ground, and the more human thought of God as the Father. As Ground, God is not the same as the universe, but is the ultimate centre of the power which the universe manifests. As Father, God is not identical with His sons, yet is in an intimately personal sense the source of their life.

What is all this reasoning but the confession that the eternal Father is in a sense transcendent, above our knowledge and experience; but is at the same time the intelligible basis of precisely these familiar experiences with which our inquiry began? No attempted logic is more absurd than the endeavour to prove the existence of God, yet no language is so inadequate as that which omits the divine transcendence. The very limitation of all attempts to prove that God exists is a profound revelation of His presence. We need not prove that which is the Ground of proof. We need only state the existence of the Uncaused. But having found Him, it were folly to erect any barrier to our thinking. If no account describes God adequately, no description leaves Him wholly out. The Ground of all knowing is by very nature knowable.

If God is transcendent, then, He is no less truly immanent. Whatever He may be as the absolute Reality, He is known to us in part as the God of our life, and the Source of our world. While, then, in one sense there can be no time and no space to an omnipresent Reality, in a very real sense there is time and space, since it is through His world of external manifestation that His wisdom and power are made known. Moreover, it is as necessary to conceive of His existence as immanent in, rather than as identical with His world of manifestation, as it is to distinguish His transcendence from our own knowledge of His love and wisdom. Thus we avoid the pitfalls of pantheism and mysticism, and preserve in strictly theistic terms the thought of God as the Father.

It is the empirical aspect of pantheistic utterances that is of value, not the doctrine that God and nature, or God and the soul are one. The experience of the presence of God has been a very real fact all through the ages. Hence the rhapsodies and poetic effusions of the mystics are in a sense religiously true, that is, in so far as they are regarded as descriptions of experience. But pantheism is poor philosophy, and mysticism is not ethics. When it is a question of what is real, what is true and what is right, one must turn from mere description to rational thought. The revelation of God in the realm of reason is far superior to the mere revelation of immediate feeling. The pantheists meant to utter something noble and true, but it has remained for the Christian theist really to express it. The Father-son relationship is the great fact. It is the upward look, the worship, the reverence that truly finds the Father—not the mystical merging of all that is beautiful into a vague whole. Hence the vast superiority of the revelation which makes God known as love.

It is not, then, the argument for God's existence that avails. It is not the mere theory, for that may be untrue to the supreme facts. It is the life, the love, the experience. He who can appreciatively suggest the relationship of the soul in the act of worship, in the fulness of love, is the one who most truly lays the foundations of theology, Only by persistently returning to the firsthand experience, and by repeatedly correcting the account of that experience, may one hope to overcome the artificial speculations which have separated men from God.

The profoundest religious tendency of our age is the growing conviction that the empirical revelation is the Supreme revelation. Every advance in this direction means the breaking down of the barriers which once speculatively sundered heaven and earth. As heaven is brought nearer, man's conduct necessarily changes. For it is no longer possible to masquerade as a Christian by simply believing in a speculative Deity. One must show that one has found the real God by manifesting His love in daily life. Hence experience inspires experience, and the whole religious outlook is changed. The peace "which passeth understanding" is made known through the serenity which then and there exhibits it.

But in theory, too, it is the empirically immediate revelation that is now the chief ground of argument. It is the thought of the divine immanence which above all other modern conceptions transfigures the philosophy of the age. Indeed, some theologians go so far as to say that all previous doctrines were "a mere assertion" of God's existence; it is evolution that proves His life and wisdom and power. Previous theories were content with vaguely general statements; it is the thought of God as immanent which makes the conception concrete. Hence the tendency is to look immediately within and behind the minute details of events, even as they pass, to find their Ground and Life. The entire argument of the foregoing pages points to this conclusion.

We have from the first emphasised the immanent empirical factor. The experience of the moment must be understood in the light of its immediate environment, and this environment is part of a larger whole. Event is linked to event, everything is related. The only activity we know is the activity that is just now accomplishing some end, the power that has brought the present out of the past. There is no reason to conceive of any power, life, or reality, other than the Being which the actualities of existence logically demand. All power is known by what it does, and all reality by what appears.

It would now seem absurd, then, to argue that God impressed His energy upon the primeval nebulous mass, and then retired we know not where; or that He made the world out of nothing in six days, then interfered with it from time to time by miraculous providences. For there is no need of an extra-mundane Deity. Evolution, not creation, is the law of life. The manifold changes which have brought the world to its present state, the endless working of force against force, of animal against animal, and man against man, the vicissitudes of human history, are probably as important and require the divine presence as much as the impulse which first brought our world into being—if there ever was a beginning.

Either, then—note the alternative—God put forth His own life in the world, and is immanent yet transcendent, is present in it, transforming it in this age as truly as in the irrevocable ages of the past, or there is no God. Let me repeat. Either God is revealed through the cohesive force which holds matter together, and holds the planets in their positions in space, through the love which draws man to man, and the fortunes and misfortunes which characterise his progress, through the insensible gradations by which our politics are changing and our own conflicts are making us true men and women, or there is no divine Father. For the true Father is the God of experience, the Supreme Reality which experience reveals, which makes experience possible, He is the God of action, the God of the concrete. It is our own concrete experience that makes God's presence known. God is not the same as our experience. He is not identical with the world. But the world is from moment to moment real by virtue of His immanent presence.

Life, then, ultimately speaking, is a continuous, divine communication. There is no real separation between our souls and the Father in whom, in the most literal sense, " we live and move and have our being." All nature reveals God—the sea, the sky, the mountains, the complex life of great cities, the simple life of the country, the admiration of the poet, the thought and feeling of all men, all nations, all books, all churches, all religions. All thinkers, all artists and lovers of the beautiful, are "feeling after" Him.

God, then, is revealed in nature, yet He is more than nature can manifest. He is Person, yet in a sense is beyond personality as we ordinarily conceive of it. On the one hand, He is the omnipresent power which all forces exemplify, the source of the substance which all forms contain, the basis of life whereby all beings exist. Yet He is more than this, He is Spirit, Intelligence, apprehended rather by the supreme insight of the soul than through objective experience. He is Power, yet also Love; the Author of the total universe, yet near enough so that Jesus, most truly of all, named Him "Father" in a particularly personal sense. His complete nature is made known, if at all, in the total universe. Yet He is as genuinely knowable in human life. Hence God is at once Spirit without form, and the Essence which all forms reveal, the all-loving Father who is unknown and unperceived in this larger and deeper sense, except by those who have thought and suffered deeply, He whom we refuse to recognise when we look afar into the heavens for a god of our own fancy; who is not only immanent, but who is also independent of that in which He dwells; the Friend who is as near to us in the present moment as in the countless aeons of eternity, of which this fleeting moment is a part.

Do we realise what this nearness means, what it is to dwell with God consciously? Let me try to bring Him yet nearer.

Sometimes one seems to look far into the eyes of a friend and to see the soul gazing from unseen depths in return; and, as the face softens into a smile, one draws still nearer to that elusive somewhat called "the human spirit," as it lends life and beauty to the features, itself invisible, yet so plainly revealed that one can almost locate its vanishing touch. There are days in the country in summer—noticeably in June and September—when a divine stillness seems to rest over all the world. We feel an unwonted and indescribable peace which lifts us above our petty selves to the larger Self of eternal restfulness which nature's calm suggests. We almost worship nature at such a time, so near it brings us to the Spirit which imbues the very vibrations of the atmosphere. Again, when standing near some grand mountain, or when looking far into the clouds at sunset, we seem to perceive the strength and the vanishing glory of Him who is almost revealed to our longing eyes, yet forever remains beyond our keenest physical vision.

If we push our analysis still farther, we discover that all that is best and dearest in human life, all that is most useful in nature, is like this retreating beauty of a soft landscape: the mechanism is visible, the beauty is of the mind. "I saw my friend," you say. Yet you saw only his face, not his soul, as you see the world, but not the Life which animates it. You feel love, you use wisdom, you reap the inner benefits of goodness; but all is intangible. No one ever saw force: we see and make use of its effects. Yet no one doubts its existence. We know it through its manifestations. Some thinkers affirm that there is no dense material, simply varied modes of motion of one force, while other philosophers describe the universe as a system of ideas produced in us by the great Reality behind all phenomena. Whatever the ultimate nature of matter may be, it is evident that the Reality is made known to us through these phenomena.

The retreating beauty of nature, then, seems typical of our deepest associations with the Father, a union to which Emerson has given expression in his Over-soul. We are conscious of the human part; and, when in times of sorrow we seem comforted from on high, we are dimly aware of the divine. Yet we cannot fully grasp it: we can only affirm that God resides in and is the supreme source of our being, as the grandeur of nature resides in a landscape whose beauty we can never locate. Take love, take wisdom, start with any quality in human life which points to a common nature, and, tracing it to its source, one's thought is lost in contemplation of the great Reality which is revealed through all these qualities, since there could be but one central love and wisdom, which all share in greater or lesser degree, as surely as the force with which I move my arm is related to the power which, from all time, has caused the planets to revolve.

Were we not thus intimately related to the Father, there would be some place where He does not exist. Unless our activity is ultimately connected with His life, there is an existence independent of Him. Our life, our consciousness must then in the ultimate sense have its being in His life, however separate from that life in a relative sense it may be. Since our being is thus grounded, we are even more dependent on Him than the plant is upon the sunlight. Moreover, since God must be conscious in order thus to be the basis of our being in the highest sense, He evidently knows and possesses us as parts of the universe of His manifestation. Thus from many points of view the fact of the divine presence is brought home to us, we recognise that despite our finitude we especially reveal God whenever we love and serve, when we are really wise. Hence it is apparent that while we possess a life of our own, in a sense we have no existence apart from Him.

In such a realisation, namely, that we are intimately related in consciousness and in love with the ever-renewing Life, and that we reveal more and more of the divine nature as we ascend in the scale of being, lies a real way of escape from morbid self-interest, introspection, self-consciousness, want of confidence, the sense of one's insignificance. To know that our highest love, our deepest thought, our truest self, is not wholly our own, but, in so far as it is unselfish, is divine—this it is to have a principle in which we can trust, which shows us what we are, not as weak human beings whom we vainly try to understand by self-analysis, but what we are as individual manifestations of the divine nature. Thus the painful thought is lost in the consciousness of divine nearness, as though a particle of sunlight should become aware of its relation to all sunlight and to the sun. What a pleasure it is to view nature and human life with an ever-deepening consciousness of this divine background! Truly, there is no ground for complaint if we dwell in this pure region of thought where we regard all activity as founded upon the divine life, where the landscape suggests the beauty which it so well typifies.

From all this it is clear that there is a vast difference between the worship of God as manifested through nature and the pantheistic identification of God with nature. Nature, thus regarded, is the realm of fact, the given sphere of experience. The thought of the divine beauty is the value attributed to nature by idealistic consciousness. It is philosophy, not physical observation, which enables us to find God in nature. It is aesthetic intuition, combined with religious aspiration, not mere sense-perception, through which the apprehension of the divine presence occurs.

Likewise in the subjective world, it is necessary to distinguish between religious emotion and the idealisation of such emotion. God is not an object of sensuous apprehension but an object of insight. The mere fact of religious fervour at any given moment counts for very little; it is the accumulated values of such experiences which in due time lead to their inferential use. The moment's experience is no doubt profoundly real, but it requires acute analysis to discover the multiform inferences which we read into it. Again, the illusions are such that one must carefully distinguish the dualities of self and the play of moods, as we shall see more clearly in other chapters.

When all discriminations have been made, it is the thought of the divine love which most sanely guides the soul. In the attitude of love, reverence, worship, the sense of sonship is too strong to permit the mind to make the customary mystical inferences. It is clear that even a perfect Being could hardly exist without an object of love, distinct from himself. If there is such distinctness, there are other Father-son relationships, also. Hence there is a reason for the existence of human beings, and for the existence of nature, as the theatre of their activity. The mutations of the world of manifestation and interaction thus supply objects of the divine consciousness. Something is being accomplished in the world. The divine life is not a bare monotony. Hence we may say that only through His own progressive life-process is God made perfect. The love of God is made complete through its complete realisation. Through our own love we share in the creative love of the Father.

As abstract as this reasoning may seem, it suggests the great fact that even in God's life there is mental activity akin to ours, that God reveals Himself in detail through the world of finite life, through human aspiration, as well as in human struggle. For a divine need is met in our lives. We fulfil a larger purpose while we realise our own. This need not imply a purpose in the older theological sense. For there may be no hard-and-fast world-plan, there may never have been a world-beginning in the sense once conceived. But there is at least mutual relationship, and hence neither human nor divine purposes may be understood alone.

In order to suggest this wholeness of relationship of the great world-order, let us once more adopt the imperfect figures of human speech, and conceive of God as a marvellously wise, all-loving Thinker, in whose comprehension the shining worlds of space and the tiniest stems are grouped in one system of self-realisation; through whose measured reflection are evolved planets such as our own, unvarying in their law because He is unchangeable, requiring ages of time because His reflection is measured and sure, definite in shape and known to us as matter because His purpose is rational; and through whose tender care we are led onward to conscious union in thought and deed with His purpose for us. Our earth, then, is a part of the great rational life of God. It has its definite orbit and a definite history; it follows unchanging laws because it is part of His thoroughly rational life. It is distinct from other spheres of the supreme activity, because its history fulfils a specific purpose. It is finite, because it is a part only of this rational life. Thus, also, you and I are expressions of the omnipresent Life, yet are finite because God means one thing in your life, and something else in mine. We are imperfect, incomplete, because we join with others to form His meaning; and He has not yet developed our lives to their perfect conclusion.

Such a figure, although it involves many speculative difficulties, seems most nearly to approximate the nearness which human speech can barely suggest. I am trying to show that God knows us, even though we fail to know Him, that He has a purpose with us which He is even now executing, that He is the completing Self without whom our lives have little meaning; the Knower and the possessor of the known; the Sustainer and the love which sustains; and the Limiter whose will we know as "law," without whom we are as naught, with whom as gods.

In those rarest moments of human life when the soul, in the peaceful isolation of the woods, by the sea, or in the quiet of the library, is lifted above itself and made aware of its kinship with the Father, have you not been conscious of just such relationship as this? Has not God seemed for the moment to belong to you alone, as though in the unsearchable depth of His love He lived for you? Yet were you not conscious that the Spirit which then moved you to silence is the same which speaks throughout the countless spheres of the universe? What a divine joy would life be could we always maintain this consciousness of the divine presence! But are we not apt to forget this nearness, to fear, to worry, and to act as though we were quite independent of the great Father, without whom we could not be?

What is life for, in the deeper sense, if it be not for the development of this higher consciousness? Is it not in our moments of earnest thought when we reflect on experience and learn its meaning, that we grow? If men were judged on the basis of real worth, would not so much avail as we really are as thinking, helpful souls—that part of us which survives all change?

Man may figuratively be called a point of energy, a centre of application of divine Power. His consciousness, his will, if he is aware of his eternal birthright, is a vantage-point whence the infinite Thinker views the world and thereby knows Himself. But God seems to act through the majority of men almost by force, for they seem unaware of His presence. They are moved in throngs, and spurred along by suffering, because in their short-sightedness they fear and oppose the moving which is for their deepest good. As Emerson puts it, "We are used as brute atoms until we think, then we use all the rest." Yet, if this world-order is the wisest system the love of God must be as clearly manifested in the struggles which carry us onward until we think as in our moments of repose. It is character that avails, that is the purpose of our contests; and character is the result of determined effort to surmount the obstacles we are compelled to meet. The experiences of evil and suffering seem in a sense to be entirely justified by the good which is brought out of them—although this does not make evil good.

Without contrast and comparison we could not interpret experience. Without darkness and evil we should not know light and good, even if we were perfect at the start, since our perfection, like that of a God without manifestation, would simply be an unrealised ideal. It is the one who has lived and suffered, conquered, thought, and practised his theories, who moves with the divine law. He is no longer as one among thousands, but is himself a mover, a sharer of power, co-operating in intelligent companionship with the Father. Then dawns the Christ-consciousness, with its accompanying life of service; and the faithful soul enjoys a more personal relationship with God, whom he now knows through actual experience to be literally the God of love.

But our realisation of the immanence of God must do more for us than simply to furnish a rational basis for belief in omnipresent Reality. Mental freedom and lasting benefits come from systematic thinking about life, as well as inner repose, when we have pushed through to settled conviction. But the real test of faith comes in times of trouble and periods of discouragement. If we say that we believe in God, and then worry, doubt, fear, and return to our selfish life, we do not yet possess the omnipresent Comforter. To act as though we really believed that God is in His world, in our souls, concerned in our daily experiences, ready to strengthen us in any need whatsoever—this is a genuine test of faith. To lift our thoughts to Him habitually, not periodically, as if we really expected help, instead of asking for the impossible—this is genuine prayer.

Do we put our faith to such a test? Do we try to trust God fully, understandingly, with a deep conviction that it is His life, His power, that is pressing upon us through our inmost life? Do we wait for guidance when we are perplexed? Do we try to see the divine meaning, the outcome of our experience as part of a great world-experience? Do we let life come as it may from the divine source, without rebellion, without doubt, carrying before us an ever-renewed ideal of ourselves as possessing some meaning in the divine economy? Do we turn from matter to the Reality behind it; from the body to the soul; from the appearances which seem so real to the life which these phenomena reveal?

I am not asking these questions from the point of view of mere theory. There are earnest souls who make this practical realisation of the immanence of God the basis of a system of everyday conduct, the basis of solution of all practical problems. Nor am I advocating mere faith, or the easy-going optimism which assures men that all will come out well, whatever they do. I am pleading, first, for a rational interpretation of experience; second, for the conception of a supreme Reality competent to give continuous life to this world; and, finally, for wise adjustment to and intelligent co-operation with the tendencies which spring from within. I advocate that interpretation of life which places the responsibility largely upon ourselves; which teaches us not to lean on systems of thought and on people whom we permit to do our thinking for us, but encourages us to look within to find the ever-present resource.

The wise attitude of adjustment we shall consider more in detail in other chapters. Here it suffices to point out that if creation is continuous, we may well believe in immanent activities which will guide the man who discovers them. Obviously, the ultimate test of our belief in the immanent God is its effect upon conduct. It makes all the difference, then, what values we associate with the divine presence. Whether we conclude that there is actual divine prompting, or that the creative instinct indicates the power of our own latent individuality, the result is practically the same; for it is through this individuality that God works. God does not speak to us "out of the air"; He inspires us through what we are doing. That is precisely the lesson of our study. We are no longer to look for the Father in the general, the vague, the mystical; we should find Him in the concrete. Hence there is need to give specific attention to the kind of mental life that best reveals the divine presence. Hence there is new reason for faith and for practical trust.

The impression prevails that trust plays a small part in the rational life. Yet reflection shows that our conduct is in large part dependent on it. The reputation of a business house may be ruined in an hour, if its standing is seriously questioned and the report is noised about. With all that science has told us about nature's laws, we are still compelled to take the world on trust. We fall quietly asleep at night, believing that the day will dawn tomorrow, that no calamity will befall our world, that it will be safe to depend on nature's forces. Nature has never deceived us, and we believe she never will. Yet we do not know what may happen. We run a thousand risks each day, in the streets, in the cars, everywhere, with perfect composure. May we not carry our trust a bit farther and understand that on which we should rely? Is God less watchful, is He any less present in the realm of thought? If gravitation holds the earth in its position in space, may it not be that its spiritual counterpart, the love of God, sustains our souls in their progress, and provides for us in ways which we have scarcely suspected? Yet how many of those who say, "God is love," stop to realise the world of meaning in that little sentence?

Whatever place the conception of God as transcendent plays in theistic philosophy, the poetic conception of the going forth of the creative spirit, or love, makes the divine immanence concrete for us in a wonderfully practical way. To regard the creative spirit as immanent and continuous is to acknowledge that all along the way the divine love cares for man. It is no mere figure of speech that describes the world as embosomed in the divine love. It was that love which brought us forth. It is through that love that the purpose of the divine wisdom is realised. Again, it is through the expression of love that man rises to the level of communion with the Father. Hence it is important to make the fact of love-relationship the basis of the most concrete realisation of the immanence of God.

For example, to conceive of the divine spirit going forth in the form of love is to see that in a sense there is not the least separation between the Father and our individual selves. The thoughts of "power," "substance," "life," still leaves us with a sense of separateness. When we apprehend the divine love we attain at last the realisation of fatherhood. We see that there is literally no barrier between, no substance, no space, to keep us from the Fatherly care. Hence we feel and know that we exist with the Father in a relationship typified by that of a child in its mother's arms. He is our Father, though transcendent in power and wisdom. Nothing can prevent us from enjoying His love, His help, His peace and inspiring guidance, except our own failure to recognise His presence. Let us, then, be still and know His love and indwelling presence. Let us test it fully, and learn what it will do for us if we never worry, never fear, never reach out away from this present life. Let us absorb from His love as the plant absorbs from the sunlight; for our spirits, like the plants, need daily nourishment.

Can we estimate the value of such reflection as this, if renewed day by day? Sometimes a text of Scripture, a poem, or a piece of music, will quicken it in us. Sometimes we must seek the solitude of nature where the Spirit comes; for it is the Spirit that is the essential, not any form of words, or suggestions. Silently and unobserved, the Spirit will breathe upon us if we reflect, if we wait for it in stillness day by day. It will not come if doubt, if we fear, or—note this especially—if our thought is too active; for the Spirit never intrudes. It lets us go our way if we choose: it comes, we hardly know how, if we trust. All it asks is receptive listening. Then all that an unselfish human being would wisely ask is ours.

It steals into our consciousness when we think deeply, to guide, to strengthen, to encourage. The great secret of life is to know how, in our own way, to be receptive to it, how to read the message of its inner whispering. The sure method of growing strong in realisation of its nearness is to believe that it will come if we listen, to trust it in moments of doubt as the lost hunter trusts his horse in the forest. It will come if we have an ideal outlook, then renew our realisation day by day, ever remembering that, as the Spirit is the Supreme Reality, we live in it, and with it, and there is naught to separate us from its everwatchful care, its ever-loving presence.

Chapter III
The World of Manifestation

—

ONE truth was clear at every stage in the foregoing discussion. Every atom, every event, every soul in the universe is imbued with the immanent Presence—life is a constant sharing of divine power. Whatever be the starting-point in our interpretation of experience, whether in some truth of the reason, some cherished insight of the inner life, or a fact in the outer world, there is no stopping-place short of the conclusion that God is the immanent Reality, the sufficient Ground of all existence. We may evade the point or deviate into agnosticism, by giving undue regard to the limitations of finite consciousness. But our deepest nature is never satisfied until we attain a conception which meets the ultimate needs of thought.

To be sure, we found it necessary to distinguish between a logical argument for the ultimate Ground of things, and the thought of God as the object of religious consciousness. We discarded all formal attempts to prove that God exists, and rejected the popular argument from causation. But this presented no difficulty, since we are not here so much concerned with the philosophical idea of Ground, with the idea of God as transcendent, as with the immanent relation between God and His world. The modern thought of nature and of human experience demands that relationship at every point, without regard to time or space. Yet to find God in everything, is not to conclude that one finds only God. The experiences of the inner life are the severest tests. For if we are able to maintain the reverential attitude of sonship we may enter into the divine love with all joy, yet avoid the pitfalls of mysticism. Finally, we betray our real belief by what we do. To trust, to be profoundly faithful, is indeed to show that the divine immanence is a reality in our lives. By its fruits shall the degree of our love be known.

The adjustment of the inner life to the thought of God is thus the first great step in the present inquiry. The mere argument, the theory of the divine immanence, is secondary. The essential is the attitude we adopt, the effect upon conduct. Unless we make this profoundest of all adaptations, we cannot expect to enter into the fulness of the other two great relationships, the adjustment to nature and to man. To regard nature, for example, in the light of the divine immanence is to take a vastly different view from that of ordinary thinking.

It is the custom, nowadays, to trace the immanent connections of things, to look back of each event to its immediate physical environment as its cause. This line of inquiry is doubtless in the right direction. But it is apt to stop short of the profoundest interests in human life. The ideal of mechanical science is to describe every event in terms of exactly measurable forces, and it is doubtless a convenient fiction to regard nature as an independent, self-operating mechanism. Yet it is important to bear in mind the entire inadequacy of this working hypothesis. Above the realm of the mechanical there is the domain of the organic and the realm of the conscious. The mechanical principle is strained to the utmost to make it include the organic, and within certain limits it is no doubt applicable. This partial success should not, however, blind us to the fact that there is a higher order of existence where all quantitative explanations fail, where thought must turn from the measurable to the qualitative, and from what merely is to what ought to be.

The aim of the present chapter is not to propound a complete theory of nature, but to make certain observations which bear on our interpretation of the inner life. From the point of view of ultimate values, the physical universe is not the total universe, but is the most objective, outer portion of the divine order. The highest type of reality is spiritual. The fundamental character or constitution of things is grounded in the intelligence, the being and love of God. Only by reference to their fundamental environment may things be understood. Hence the visible world is not comprehensible alone. It is not even a system or unity of law-exemplifying forces, by itself. Nature possesses system through its relation to the total divine order. Hence it is the home of man in other than a merely physical sense, and it should be regarded in the light of all the ideals to which man's earthly life contributes. That which gives it its seemingly independent life is the aspiring Spirit which went forth from God into manifesting activity, and is mounting through all the levels of mechanical forces and organic life to the moral and spiritual plane.

The old-time thought of God as the creator of something out of nothing is still so strong that when one proposes to consider the world as a manifestation, the question arises, What is the purpose of this divine self-revelation? That the world reveals God is almost a truism. But the question is, Why does God thus reveal Himself? The answer may be regarded as the simplest or the most difficult problem that can be asked in regard to the world of nature. It is easy to argue that God created the world according to "design." The facts of nature everywhere suggest such an argument. But modern thought has little need of the notion of a designer. Theological arguments of that kind are quite out of fashion. If the universe has always existed in some form, there never was a beginning, hence no "creation" and hence no "design." The attempts to assign a purpose for creation have been rather puerile. Wiser men have been contented with the profound suggestion that the world came forth from the "fulness" of the divine nature. It was not due to any imperfection on His part that God created the world. He was not compelled to create it. But in His abounding love he freely sent Himself forth.

We may say, then, that the world reveals the nature of God—in so far as physical forms and evolutions can manifest Him. There seems no reason to allege that there ever was a time when God did not reveal Himself in objective form. The world as a system is of a certain character because God is of a certain nature. The world exists, that is the chief fact. Granted the world, we may if we please say that its purpose is to reveal the being of God in objective form. The world as a fact is one thing, the world as said to exemplify values is another. What values the divine Father may see in it, only the Father can tell. The values you and I find in it depend upon the state of development we have attained, the theory of life we hold. It would be absurd for any man to insist that his scheme of values exhausts the purposes of life.

The question of purposes, then, is subordinate to the question of character. What is the nature of the world? What are its laws? How is it constituted as a whole? What has been its history? What seem to be its tendencies? Such questions immediately resolve themselves into innumerable inquiries in regard to different aspects of nature, and it is the province of the special sciences to answer these questions. What most concerns us is the character of human existence in the natural world. Here again the inquiry divides and subdivides. It matters greatly where we chanced to be born, what our racial interests are. It is remarkable what a chaos of values, what confused notions exist in regard to man's place in nature. It is obviously of far greater consequence to determine the general nature of the conditions and laws of physical existence, and leave the problem of particular values for later consideration.

It was once customary to contrast the realm of nature with "the realm of grace," to the entire disparagement of man's natural life. Then came the reaction against the supernatural, and nowadays the reaction has gone so far that the tendency is to overlook the values and realities that are more than natural. A more rational philosophy would doubtless see ends in nature considered as if nature were independent, and lines of development which have a natural beginning but reach far into the invisible. It is convenient, for example, to speak of the conservation of natural energy while we are not attempting to state what that energy is or what end it subserves. As a relative end in itself, nature possesses a beauty, a worth which needs no ulterior sanction. Many ideals of a mechanical and organic character doubtless reach perfection in nature. As the home of physical man, as the embodied expression of mental and social life, nature is relatively complete. The ephemeral, temporal ends attained in animal life are surely of real and almost independent worth. Quite apart from all the woes and calamities which constitute nature's darker history there is much to be said about these subordinate ends, and nature is far from existing for man's sake alone. The naturalism, the poetry and mythologies which recognise these earthly beauties are permanent possessions of human literature.

Among many other things, nature makes for variety, endurance, strength, and health as physical ends of priceless value. The fact that man has made miserable use of his opportunities should not be emphasised at the expense of the profound thought of what man might have been, of what he may yet be. It is as unfair to charge nature with human woes as to disparage her because of her subordinate position. A vast amount of subjectivism must be brushed away before we shall really begin to see nature as she is. From the days of the crudest polytheism and animism to the days of orthodox salvation schemes the tendency has been to read speculative notions into nature. Even now there are those who insist that the physical cosmos is far less orderly than modern science claims.

The first essential, then, is to recognise that as part of the self-revelation of God nature possesses a character quite independent of the thought and conduct of men. To understand that character we should look, not to human speculation and subjectivity, but to nature regarded as it exists for all and as grounded in the being of God. It is to the lasting credit of modern science that it is making the most persistent effort to differentiate between nature and human prejudice.

The second need is to regard nature in such wise that we shall see its place in human experience, side by side with the inner life. In short, it is as important to give nature its due with respect to our spiritual life as to avoid the mystic identification of nature with God. Whatever its ultimate reality and worth, and however incomplete our natural existence may be, nature is in relation to man a world of matter, of things and forces which exist independently of his mere thinking about them. Furthermore, the relation of God to matter is in a sense as intimate and direct as His relation to the human soul. We cannot deny the existence of matter. To make such a denial would be to assert the non-existence of a part of the character and purpose of God, as well as of the world of all that we physically experience. Yea, to deny it is blasphemy.

It is true, the world of matter which you and I perceive may have no objective existence precisely as we perceive it. Science tells me that certain ether waves impinge on my retina, and form an image, which in turn is translated into an idea, and interpreted according to my education. Certain other rays indirectly produce perceptions in your mind, and are interpreted according to your conceptions. The external object may be the same in both cases; but the conceptions which represent it may be quite different. I never see exactly the same object which you contemplate, nor do we as minds actually see the object at all, since we know the object by means of ideas. We are unable even to dissociate the actual sensation and the perception based on a lifetime of experience and thought by which we interpret it. Nor do we hear the same sound, perceive the same colours, or smell the same odours. But the existence of something real which causes the sensations no one can seriously question. Even an uninterpreted sensation makes us partially aware of something not ourselves. We may be scientifically aware that the sensation is in and not outside of our minds, and that we interpret it through ideas; but the object that produces the sensation is not necessarily an idea. When the hand encounters a masonry wall, we are sure of the existence of an external force which meets and effectually withstands all the pressure we are able to exert.

Despite the fact that the ultimate character of nature is not discoverable by physical science, nature proves to be a relatively uniform system everywhere exemplifying the same laws and forces. Nature is not a collection of fragments, of warring atoms, but possesses a certain order, harmony. The forces which we ordinarily speak of as distinct, such as heat, light, electricity, are transformable into one another. One force in varying modes of motion is the underlying physical principle. That force can neither be physically created nor destroyed, but is constantly conserved.

Some scientific men have been inclined to describe the uniformity of nature as atomic, that is, the order thus far attained by nature is attributed to the systematic arrangement of atoms, an arrangement which came about through fortuitous play and impact. This view dates back to Leucippus and Democritus, and it was long the prevailing hypothesis of those who fought the notion of "design" in nature and contended for a mechanical, quantitative explanation of things.

The mechanical theory has by no means been abandoned. But it seems more and more improbable that atoms are the ultimate elements of all being. Recent discoveries have pointed to the conclusion that radiant energy in various forms is the primal physical force of all that we denominate "substance," "elements," and the like. It may be that modes of motion in the ether are the final activities with which physical science has to deal. Such activities may still be describable in quantitative terms. The more simple, relatively independent the description of nature becomes, the more serviceable will be such description alike for the physical scientist and for the philosopher. The attempt to carry the mechanical hypothesis as far and as high as possible is not to be deplored but to be welcomed. It is the physical scientist who is alone able to develop the great idea of the uniformity of nature, for it is he alone who possesses the essential facts. It is only a question of secondary details. The conception of uniformity is now well-established. If the secondary details and the discoveries of new elements point to a higher conception than the purely mechanical theory, the physical scientist will be the first to acknowledge it.

As a matter of fact, it is one of the profoundest achievements of nineteenth-century science that it has gradually passed beyond the merely mechanical theory which had such vogue after the great discoveries of Galileo, Kepler, and Newton. Popular thinking has scarcely risen as yet to the modern biological point of view. We are still inclined to think and speak of matter as "inert" or "dead." Science shows us that it is nowhere inert, not even in the great rock foundations of our earth. Physical death is only a state of transition to another form of life. It is life that is fundamental, not what is popularly called a "thing," or "substance." The word "substance" is ordinarily applied as if each table, house, rock, were a thing by itself, a permanent entity, or unitary mass. But science points out that there are everywhere mutations of life, even in the apparently most solid body. The term "matter" is simply a general expression for relatively mobile forms of life in various grades from the seemingly lifeless granite through less compact forms, solids, liquids, gases, and the attenuated nerve tissues which approach the nature of mind. Furthermore, a single substance—for instance, water—passes successively through three states, as a solid, as liquid, and as vapour, the integration and disintegration of matter in various forms being one of the most striking phenomena of material life. Even the earth's atmosphere has been reduced to liquid and solid forms. The chemical process called combustion is capable of liberating in an incredibly short space of time all the solid materials of a vast building, and transforming them into invisible gases, leaving only a heap of ashes to attest the ruin. Nothing is stable in material form, nothing can resist the subtle, invisible activities of the one force, interpenetrating the seemingly immutable forms of matter, setting the particles into rapid vibration, or causing them to appear in ever-varying combinations.

Nature is not only the theatre of laws and forces, but is, figuratively speaking, a live organism. That is, the term "organism," as inadequate as it is, suggests an aspect of nature which the word "mechanism" fails to exemplify. Of this great throbbing thing of life physical man is a part, so closely related to it that he seems to be the central figure whose existence was prophesied from the very dawn of being.

To make this relationship clear, think for a moment what this great natural existence means. In an organism no part is complete in itself, but supplements and depends on all the other parts. No part can in itself be perfect, since it would then be a separate organism. The cog-wheel may be a truly wonderful contrivance; yet it is useless unless it exactly fits into some machine which is incomplete without it. The musical note, however pure, has no meaning for us unless it is sounded in unison with others.

The same is true of man. He cannot live in isolation. He is not good alone. He must have a particular gift or occupation, in order that perfection may be attained by the whole. He is a dependent being, and in turn contributes his little share of benefit. Countless ages elapsed before he could exist at all, and every one of the innumerable hosts that preceded him lived and struggled that he might be born. From those who labour day by day come the food, the clothing, and the homes which make continued life possible. Numberless thousands of minds have thought out and formulated that which today constitutes our knowledge of art, science, history, literature, and philosophy; and the largest contribution to our knowledge made by a single mind seems wonderfully small, our own original thought infinitesimally smaller. Each of these incidental forces in the worlds of nature, of society and thought, about which we think so rarely, contributes its share to the shifting series of experiences called life, each plays its part in the great organism.

The most important fact remains. This beautifully organised thing of life, with its wonderful law-governed parts and its co-operation of beings and things, was not made suddenly or out of hand. It has grown out of that which has probably existed eternally. Slowly, as the seed matures in the ground and prepares the way for the bursting bud and the blooming plant, everything in nature, so far as we know, from the raising of continents to the development of man, has taken place and reached its present condition by insensible degrees. Today is the product of yesterday, and yesterday of the day before, and so on indefinitely. Each cause is the effect of another cause more remote. The life of the tree comes from the sun millions of miles away, but it comes through something. Its energy is stored in the organic and inorganic materials immediately surrounding the tree, and through the heat and light transformed from the solar rays by the earth's atmosphere. The immediate environment, ancestry, and experience give rise to all living things; and all life finds its origin in a single environment. Evolution is the only law yet discovered which in any way accounts for the origin of our world in its present form. When one pauses to consider what this law is as a universal principle, it becomes evident that there could be no other.

Yet it is easy to misunderstand this principle. To many evolution simply means the derivation of man from some lost ancestor, a belief which generally arouses a feeling of repugnance; for it means that the existence of God is not necessary under this theory, and one naturally lays it aside as irreligious. Yet evolution would be of little significance if it were not a universal law, as well exemplified in the growth of the tree as in the development of new species or of a planet from a mass of nebula. It would have no ultimate meaning unless it proved the presence of God at every step in the great world process.

In the foregoing chapter we have seen that the whole problem is simplified by the knowledge that all life is immanent, that the activity of beings and things is due to the Power resident in that which lives and grows. If God is immanent in one portion of the universe, He must be immanent in all. If He gives rise to a world and its people, He must be with the world in order for it to endure. This much is clear: it only remains to discover, as far as possible, the series or gradations of power and substance whereby Spirit makes itself known to and revealed as the lowest forms of being, and to note the successive stages through which all beings pass in their upward growth.

This latter task is the work of natural science; and year by year her workers are collecting evidence, classifying facts, inquiring into the causes of variation, the influence of environment, the effect of use and disuse, the transmission of acquired variations, and all other problems connected with development; howbeit there is still great diversity of opinion on all these points. Every fact makes our knowledge of the immanent God more concrete. Every datum supplies a link in the series of causes and effects. Every factor plays its part. Every step bears some relation to its antecedent and its consequent. And all facts, all forces, all events, are related to the entire universe.

One need only observe the social and political changes going on today, class contending with class and party with party, in order to discover every aspect of this universal principle. We forget this law sometimes, and undertake to force events, we endeavour to convince ourselves that there is a royal road to success; but we soon discover that we can omit no steps.

The seed planted in the ground, like the new idea sown in a wilderness of conflicting opinion, contains an indwelling principle of life, which causes it to develop in a certain way. It grows and absorbs nutriment from the sunlight, it matures slowly, it is dependent solely on what it has within and what closely surrounds it. Its growth may be hastened within certain limits, but only by introducing a new factor. The plant which it becomes in due time is a type of the results of all physical evolution. It is growth, not by creation out of nothing, but through the transformation of that which already exists into something different. Its growth is due to the interaction of part on part. Its transmutation into another species can only result through modification, the introduction into its life of some new element. The new element once introduced, whether in the organic or the inorganic worlds, in society, in politics, in religion, a change is sure to result.

But we have the best evidence in our own lives; and the chief problem, laying aside all discussion of particular theories of evolution, is to discover the actual course of events in daily experience, to learn how far we have gone in the upbuilding of character, how to aspire and co-operate with the immanent activities of our being.

We have an excellent example of what evolution means in the growth of ideas. We are born with a set of opinions on matters of politics, religion, and the like. There is a strong tendency toward conservatism; and we are for a time inclined to think like our parents, and even to cherish and defend the dogmas which have come down to us. But with each experience, each new book, each new acquaintance with the world and with people, which makes an impression on us, a new factor enters into our thought; and the only way to avoid progress is to avoid contact with progressive people.

So well is this understood by certain leaders of thought that they forbid their followers to read outside of established lines; for they know that, if people think, they will change. Ideas have a resident, a stimulating life, especially when they come fresh from the minds of those to whom the world's mental progress is due. They speak to us in books. They compel our assent through reason and through people. And, once sown in the mind, they work a wonderful transformation, until they burst forth with all the power of firm conviction.

Yet the transition is ever gradual and law-governed, like the growth of the tree. No idea is established without controversy. We turn it over, weigh it, and view it in all its aspects, just as new social and political institutions grow out of controversy and long experience. The power of conviction comes only when the last objection has been met. We are involuntarily as moderate and painstaking as Nature herself. If perchance we forget the natural method, and jump at conclusions, we discover no way of making them sure but to go back and supply all the steps. If an idea appeals to us at once, it is because thought and experience have already prepared the way for its acceptance. We cannot force a full-grown idea into the mind of another any more than nature can be interfered with from without. We are compelled to seek a starting-point, to discover some idea already existing in the mind of the other person, and lead on gradually from the known to the unknown. Nor can we create a new philosophy or originate any idea which has no basis in experience. Whether we will or no, we must take cognisance of universal human knowledge, and develop our thought from that. Psychology shows that even the wildest and most absurd fancies of the imagination are in some way products of experience.

Our rational self challenges us to find any method of growth and change except that of patient evolution, the great world-wide process of "continuous progressive change, according to unvarying laws, and by means of resident forces." The process once called "creation" is as long as time itself, as wide as the universe. It is going on today. It will never cease until its great task is completed. It is thorough, painstaking, gradual, and sure. It is economical, careful, and direct, making use of every incident, every possible factor, every so-called chance, so that in human life joy, sorrow, hardship, success, heredity, disposition, environment, education, society, and thought, are called into use; and all these factors have a bearing on the result. "The ideal is immanent in the real." The aspiring force speaks through the slightest incident of experience. The omnipresent Spirit aspires through, co-operates with, and seeks co-operation from the individual soul to whom it is ever trying to make itself known. God is immanent in evolution.

In order to make this intimate relationship of God and His world of manifestation clear and vivid, let us try for a moment to conceive the long series of forces and substances, interpenetrating and blending with each other, and descending from the central Love down through the various levels of manifestation to the physical and chemical forces and all the volatile substances to the liquids, solids, and finally to the hard rock. Or, starting with the nebulous mass out of which our universe is said to have developed, let us pass imaginatively upward through the vast cycles of cosmic time, the thought of which adds depth and meaning to the conception of God. Good visualisers will probably call up some mental picture which suggests these vast stretches of time. Out of the gradually cooling mass which at length takes shape as our earth they will imaginatively see the dawn of life, and the moderate, patient, purposeful transition from the inorganic to the organic kingdom, the long periods in which one form of animal life succeeded and won supremacy over another, the change from the rank vegetation of the carboniferous period to the graceful forms of today, the raising of continents and mountains, the retreat of the great ice-sheets which once covered large portions of the northern hemisphere, and the dim outlines of that far-distant society, the herding together of men, out of which grew modern civilisation.

Thus we come at last to the dawn of human history. The epochs of the past unfold before us with new meaning. We note how period has grown out of period, event out of event. Thought becomes overpowered by the vastness and complexity of civilised life in its endless phases, its manifold contributions to the arts and sciences. The great truths of religion and philosophy, the great souls of history, claim our attention at last; and thus the thought turns once more to the Supreme Reality whose ideals are the goals of this long evolution.

One's personal thought is lost in contemplation of the Universal. One is momentarily lifted above the present, above the world of human life, into the life of worlds, of the universe—yes, the very life of God, of which one seems to contemplate but one of its infinite phases. One feels that the human self is intimately related to this great Life. One communes with the Essence itself, the Spirit, the protecting Love. Matter seems like a mere symbol as compared with the worth of this ideal vision. The Life which manifested itself so long ago in the primeval history of the earth returns to consciousness in man, and recognises through him its own transcendent source. The soul knows the great unity henceforth, whatever phase of it is contemplated. It habitually turns from the universe to God and from God to His great world of manifestation.

The essential thought for our present purposes is the idea of nature as grounded in the divine order. To adjust ourselves to nature we must first consider what nature is and how it is made known. Popular notions prove to be more materialistic than scientific conceptions, for science corrects the assumption that matter is a substance by itself, inert or dead, amidst a collection of utterly different forces; and develops instead the idea of nature as living, uniform, organic. The account thus given is carried up to the point of sensation in man, yes, farther than that, for psychology as a natural science inquires into mental life in so far as it is found in close relation with the body. The mechanical explanation of things is carried as far as possible, then gives place to the biological. Biology is still more or less subservient to the mechanical theory. But a point is reached where the most important problems concerning life and mind are handed over to a higher science. Idealistic philosophy takes up the problems of nature where the special sciences leave them, critically examines all the presuppositions, and turns to the consideration of the far larger system which includes both nature and mind. Thus it is profound knowledge of the inner life that enables man truly to equip himself to adjust his life to nature. The inquiry which begins at the threshold of sensation reveals a new world.

Chapter IV
The Nature of Existence

—

IN the last chapter we were largely concerned with the world of manifestation as the domain of physical forces and natural evolution. It seemed necessary to emphasise the realities of matter and force in order to avoid the misapprehensions which arise when idealistic arguments are introduced. Moreover, only by specifically considering these realities may one adequately understand the conception of God as immanent. From one point of view, no interpretation of the divine nature is more convincing than the one which regards every detail of the physical world as immediately grounded in the life and character of God. The objectivity of God's manifestation clearly conceived, one is free to give unreserved attention to the mental world. Whatever the ultimate character of the universe, it is clear that the final system has room for nature as well as for mind. If in one sense the dualism of mind and matter is overcome in the ultimate system of relations, their union can only be intelligibly found by complete loyalty from first to last to their contrasted qualities. Hence it is well to bear in mind the magnitude of the problem. Any purely subjective theory must prove as one-sided as are all merely objective doctrines. The wisest course seems to be to consider now this phase of the world, now that, all the while endeavouring to be faithful to facts, laws, distinctions. With this purpose in mind, let us begin an entirely fresh study of the phenomena of experience.

When we look abroad in the world of life in quest of a clue to the nature of existence, we are at first inclined to describe life in material terms. So large a portion of our time is spent in providing the wherewithal to live, that occupation is naturally synonymous with philosophy.* Most of our customs and modes of speech are based on the assumption that man is a physical being. We speak of a person's face as if we really saw the individual. We even regard our bodies as ourselves. And it requires searching thought to dissociate the self from its outer garment. Of course, when we pause to think, we know that this body is not the real man. Accident may disfigure the body, but the soul is not disfigured. Endless experiences may come, in varying environments, yet it is always the same individual who perceives them. We may present many aspects or selves to different individuals, yet the same being resides behind these personalities, or masks. A man may deceive others, but he cannot be other than himself. He may be "beside himself," as the saying is, or "out of his head" in a fever. But he comes to himself again. Consciousness subsides in sleep, but that is no argument to show that it is gone, or that it is a product of the body. Man becomes insane, but it is in pursuit of an idea. Insanity does not prove a man less but more mental. And although the body ceases to be an animated whole at death, many of us expect to live in a finer world where a material body will not be needed.

That is, we do not discriminate between the appearances of things and the reality which analytical thinking would reveal. To judge by our behaviour, would no doubt be to conclude that we are materialists.

There are many lines of thought, then, which lead from the physical world to the mental. They are lines of thought,—note that. One cannot even raise the question concerning the existence of matter without turning from the body to the mind. The grossest materialist must use mental facts to argue for materialism. But, you say, he may contend that thought is a function of the brain. So it would seem. This is a common supposition, based on the presupposition that we know more about matter than about mind. This assumption lies at the basis of our habit of regarding ourselves as physical beings. The truth is that, despite our ignorance of many mental functions, we know far more about mind than about matter.

The first fact pointed out by the materialist as evidence of the existence of matter by itself is physical sensation, for example, the sensation of heat or cold. If we touch a hot stove, the hand is burned; whereas a stove without fire gives an entirely different sensation. Surely, the materialist contends, there is nothing mental about this experience. Again, the materialist might argue: I look out of the window and see yonder house, well knowing that it is at a distance from me. I can descend the stairs and walk to that house, thus proving that there is real external space, apart from the mind. Moreover, I am compelled to put my body through many successive movements, thus showing that there is time. I can touch the house, note its colour, run against it and thereby meet resistance; I cannot think it away.

Yes, I reply, the existence of temporal and spatial experience is unquestioned. The existence of sensation is equally certain, no one denies that there are differing sensations and that they are in some sense real. But the kind of reality is the point at issue. How do I happen to know that there are hot and cold substances? What makes me aware of motor experiences? How do I know that there is space? It is by comparison of mental experiences. All things were apparently spread before me as if on an immediately tangible plane surface or wall, until I began as an infant to test their relations. The simplest interpretation of space is the result of much mental experience, and it is impossible to dissociate space from the idea of it.

Yes, the materialist admits, but this is merely the training of the organism, and of course that is essential. Varied spatial experiences awaken varied ideas concerning the relationship of objects. Thus the ideas are produced by physical phenomena.

That is half of the truth, I reply, but do the varied experiences compare themselves? Do they fall into an adjustment such that I always know how to judge the connection of objects in space? What are the sensations by which I judge, and how are they known? What is the ego that feels, knows, and judges? Is that a mere automaton? The materialist is compelled to admit that the nature of the ego is unknown to him. He must admit that to touch different objects would not suffice to show that they are unequally distant from the tactual organism. This mental discovery is unlike anything the materialist can point to in the physical world. The existence of space is a discovery made by the mind. Likewise with the perception of time. A new moment does not rise up and inform me that time has elapsed since the last. Meditation on the fact of change leads to the discovery of time. So with colours, sounds, tastes, and odours. These gradually differentiate amidst the general mass of impressions which is brought in from the outside world. The colours might, it is true, have been present in some unknown form before the first wondering glance of the infant, but all that we know about them is in terms of conscious experience. They are non-existent for the infant. The material world means nothing to us without thought. Our real progress is growth in thought; without it we should never be aught more than infants. The training of the body is insignificant when compared with the training which we give the mind. This is not to say that the body does not exist, but that it is not primary in the sense ordinarily believed. Mind and body have been co-operative from the start.

The materialist talks about sensation as if there could be such a thing apart from the mind that is conscious of it. This term is as much a figure of speech as our reference to the sun as "rising" and "setting." A sensation is an impression made upon the body by a physical object or force. As hypothetically physical it is an action from outside. But how can an action from outside be felt without something to meet it from within? A sense organ meets it, in the first place, but as soon as consciousness knows it, it ceases to be a sensation, and becomes a perception, that is, a mental product. That is why sensation is in reality hypothetical; it conceivably exists, but we do not know what it is, because we have never felt one. As felt by the mind, perception is twice removed from matter regarded as external to the body. The infant is conceivably in the immediate presence of sensation, in its first moments of blurred contact with the world. But the moment the first distinction in consciousness arises the inner or mental contribution begins, and the mind is so much farther removed from matter. What the mind really contemplates is not sensation, but its own states, its consciousness of what we for convenience call "sensation." The appeal to sensation is therefore futile; for we know sensation only through consciousness.

Do you realise the full significance of this fundamental statement ? If so, and if you have hitherto looked at things from the outside, it means that you must now view them from within, that you can never again wholly view them in any other way. For note this, there is one fact from which you can never sunder your life, your experience, namely, you are conscious. Whatever else you are, whatever else life is, you are ever a conscious being; all your philosophising should begin with this fact. Whatever you know, is known in terms of consciousness. All that you feel, is consciously felt. All that you see, is perceived by the eye of the mind. For, as already noted, you do not see the retinal image; you mentally contemplate the object after it has been translated into an idea. All that you hear is a mental somewhat in some way corresponding to aural vibration. The experiences of hardness, softness, colour, temperature, light, taste, are mental. What these might be apart from your consciousness you are entirely unable to say. You might as well try to state the day and hour when time began.

There is no reason to doubt that objective activities which give rise to what we denote as sound," "sight" and the other perceptions exist, but it is pure matter of convenience to call these experiences "physical." What we mean to say, when we use words accurately, is that some of our experiences arise objectively, while others have a subjective origin. The experience which we call consciousness is awareness of relations existing between objective states and subjective states. This statement does not necessarily mean that, because I know things through mind, therefore what my mind translates for me was mind before it was translated. Nor am I, the perceiver, necessarily my own mental states, and nothing more. For as a soul, or spiritual being, my mode of contact with the world of nature may be but one type of spiritual experience.

Largely apart from the perceptual relationship with nature, I may have consciousness of a purer sort,* which may tell me more directly what the nature of existence is. It is of no avail, however, for the materialist to insist that because I cannot transcend mind I know nothing about it. I cannot define mind except in terms of consciousness; I can say no more than this: that mental states are states of the soul. But when it is a question of the contrast between mind and matter, I am able to answer the materialist's last argument by referring to the fundamental fact that, although I know but little about mind by itself, what little I do know is known in terms of consciousness.

For example, the intellectual and volitional states, the processes of rational insight.

Even so far as mind is conditioned by the brain, I am aware of those conditions only through mind. Those conditions may cease to be effective after death, but that does not imply that the mind will cease to exist, for I do not know enough about matter to affirm that it can destroy mind, and I do know enough about mind to declare that it is more fundamental, more intimately a part of me. For there is not the slightest evidence that consciousness is solely a product of the brain.

Without a brain, it is true, I probably should not have such experiences as we call "sound," "taste," " light," " heat," and the rest. But physical perception is only the lowest grade of conscious experience. Even that experience must have a percipient background. Whatever is brought forward from the physical side, it is met by a stronger fact on the mental side, in the shape of that which interprets it. There are no purely "physical" experiences without mental correspondencies; whereas there are many mental states which have no exact physical counterpart, such, for example, as our logical and mathematical processes of thought.

The sense of resistance is sometimes pointed out as purely physical, as the most fundamental evidence that the physical world exists. But all that we know about this experience is that force meets force. The materialist is unable to tell us what that force is. Moreover, resistance is not physical alone. Whose mental world is so poor that the soul has never encountered the resistance offered by fears, doubts, states of despondency and the like? What is more stubborn than one's own lower self? Again, the fact of motion is said to be primarily physical. But motion is not confined to the physical world; no moment of consciousness stands still. Consciousness is like a river where there is always a perceptible current.

You may doubt the existence of nature, but you cannot logically doubt the existence of mind. Our natural life may be a dream, but if it be "of such stuff as dreams are made of," it is all the more emphatically mental. If we shall sometime awaken to know things as they more truly are, it will probably be an awakening into a more distinct form of consciousness, where the soul is made more directly aware of what it now knows mediately. The flesh may be and doubtless is a constant source of illusion, but that is an argument for the idealist, not for the materialist. For if the mind would be freer without the body, it is all the more real; the conditions which are supposed to produce consciousness really hamper it.

Another effective argument is found in the fact that, whereas the body tends to condition the mind and man would be largely an animal if he succumbed, it is possible to triumph over the animal characteristics of the flesh and be less and less hindered by them. As powerful as are out fleshly conditions, the soul has a power whereby it can progressively transcend and transmute many of them. No analysis of physical life is capable of accounting for these progressive triumphs, this superior power. The mind tends to be unlike the flesh. It is more than the flesh. As an effect cannot be greater than its cause, we must look elsewhere than to the physical world to find the sufficient ground of all that the mind displays. That the mind awakens and displays its powers only when changing conditions furnish opportunity, is no argument in favour of matter as a cause. Matter may indeed furnish the occasion, at the outset, but there is evidence that later the soul compels the occasion.

If, now, we have really found our way into the subjective world, let us look about and take our bearings. Our argument thus far has emphasised the fact that primarily life is an affair of consciousness. We found it possible to listen to the last word of the materialist, then reply that as ponderable and real as his world is it is nevertheless known only through mind. Wherever we go, whatever our argument, from consciousness we cannot escape. This is the primary condition of life, and life is always as large for us and no larger than our consciousness. Yet to argue that consciousness is primary and, so far as we know, universal, is far from contending that it is just our consciousness and no other. The helpless babe lives in a conscious world, yet that world is brought in upon its little self through no effort of will or self-consciousness. In the early years, especially, consciousness is produced in us; it is not we who produce consciousness. Later, the soul awakens to awareness of self, discovers desires, and the power of action. These factors, as we have already said, are instrumental in bringing about changes in the flesh. Yet it is well to remember that, all through life, the changes in our consciousness are largely changes produced in us by a reality objective to our wills. We are compelled to be conscious; consciousness is given; it is not created from within. There is no mere unrelated consciousness. We build upon and modify consciousness, but it is the "stream of thought" which supplies the wherewithal. Much of the time we are little more than reflective observers.

To be conscious, then, is to live in a world. What that world might be apart from our consciousness we do not know, for we have not had the experience. Our consciousness is the translating medium through which the world is put before us in the form of ideas. It is the prime condition of existence—that is the most we can say. Wisdom obviously consists in learning as much as we can about the condition, that we may more fully reap the benefits of an existence that is given to, not chosen by, us.

I emphasise the fact that life is given, because the tendency of many who in some measure understand the power of thought is to speak as if its conditions were of our own making. If existence were merely an affair of personal thought, if thought were "omnipotent," the mind could of course create or destroy at will. There would then be in reality only this particular self; there would be no world, only this one person's subjective states; for there could not be two omnipotent powers.

To transfer the centre of power from the physical world to the mental is not by any means to try to prove it to be any less real or less the gift of the Spirit. We must continually guard against confusion between the term "thought," used in a finite, personal sense; and the term "consciousness," employed to designate the condition of life in general. Consciousness is our total experience from infancy onwards, the connection between the self, the world, and the Supreme Spirit. It is at once the world as made known and the reactions of the soul on the world, including perception, emotion, will, the rational process, desire, and the like. It is the general whole, known in childhood as a confused mass, in which various related parts are gradually noted, considered, and classified.

Thought, regarded as meditation upon this general whole, which is progressively discovered, is of course dependent, limited. It represents, symbolises, imitates, understands by contrast, comparison, and seizes upon certain phases of consciousness which it chooses to be concerned with for a time, while all else is permitted to fall into the background. It thus abstracts, it is indirect, mediate. To some of its abstractions, worshipped as truth, we owe our ages of departure from the reality of life. The concrete consciousness, on the other hand, from which these small sections of life were abstracted, was direct, immediate, and would have been a far safer guide to knowledge of reality. Thought is in a sense thrice removed from the world of reality, since it deals with remembered perceptions, or feelings, which were originally translated sense-experiences. There is every reason, then, for holding to the concrete, the first-hand experiences; and avoiding the artificial constructions of thought whereby we theoretically sunder ourselves from the world.

Moreover, as the self or soul which abides in us is more real than the thought which passes, if we were really concerned to develop a theory which should centre about the individual, we ought to put our doctrine in terms of the self, not in terms of its thoughts. The self is at once the thinker, the perceiver, and the centre of will, or attention. Although we know the soul only through what it does, through observation of ourselves as self-conscious, yet thought must take the soul into account as the prime factor. The soul and the reality whence springs the world— these are the two fundamental facts, and all our philosophising is an attempt to understand their relationships. We may then dismiss as inadequate the doctrine which undertakes to describe life in terms of thought. It is in its way as inadequate as materialism. Even consciousness, as we know it, may not be a large enough term; for both the world and the soul may be more substantial than any analysis of present consciousness reveals; and thought, at best, is only a part of consciousness.

But in dismissing the theory that thought is all-complete, we do not so readily escape from our subjectivity. One may still contend that this consciousness which I contemplate is just my consciousness, and no other. For what do I know about an alleged world existing beyond me except in terms of my own states? What do I know about you other than that which my consciousness of your relationships with me reveals? To me, the world is what I am conscious of concerning it. To me, you are what I know or think you to be. What you may be in and for yourself I do not and cannot know, for I cannot transcend my consciousness of you to acquire your consciousness of you.

Thus one might continue to accumulate arguments until, in the end, one would feel hopelessly subjective. But we may as well pause here, for if the escape from subjectivity be once made there is no going back. First let us admit, however, that there is a deep truth in these considerations. What we think and know is indeed thought and known as we apprehend it. But the fact that I know the world only as I know it does not signify that there is no world objective to myself; and the fact that I know you only as I am impressed by you does not signify that there is no self to make the impression, no "you" to know yourself intimately. I might even throw light upon your life for you, know you in part better than you know yourself, despite the fact that what I know would be known as I perceive it. The fact that I know only in an individual way is of far less consequence than that I am compelled to be conscious.

The truth, then, is that I do not need to make my escape from the subjective world. I never existed in such a world, alone. I have always been outside, that is, my most intimately self-conscious states are never purely my own. They are due to relations between myself and the world, between the soul and the Ground of all souls. Consciousness is from the start a co-operative product. The world comes to me and I slowly begin to recognise it. My soul is the centre of my world, to be sure, but I do not even discover my soul until I have discovered the world. Self-consciousness is a relatively late psychological development. I learn that I exist as a self by contrast with objects and selves external to me. The act of discovery is thus itself an objective thought, as it were. The subjective world is first known as a sort of development or projection of the objective realm. The discovery is made only as rapidly as it is possible to contrast the relatively objective with the relatively subjective.

This fine discrimination becomes clearer when stated in terms of activity. It is conceivable that the first sensation, if it could have been known by itself, would have been a sense of activity. The growing life of the physical organism reaches the point where it makes itself known.

Thus consciousness begins, the soul begins to awaken. On the physiological side, the first experience is activity, movement, life. On the mental side, it is the sensation which corresponds to activity, movement, life. The sensation itself is movement, life. A dead thing, if such there be, is not and could not be conscious. There may possibly be movement without consciousness, but there cannot be consciousness as we now know it without movement. Consciousness is awareness of change, and change implies movement. Consciousness is also a relating faculty, but new relations are perceived through the stream of consciousness. Consciousness flows, changes are produced in our consciousness by changes in our environment. To be sure, change may originate within; but I am speaking now of its earlier external origination.

What the infant possesses at the outset is not lost; self-consciousness adds to, it does not take away from. Motion or life is common to the mind and to the external world, whence come changing activities. There is no chasm to bridge between the soul and nature. From the first moment of the conceivable dawn of consciousness there was activity all along the line. There is and has been no separation. That which we know as the changing play of consciousness is on the physical side the motion or life of what we call "matter." The distinctions between the natural and conscious worlds are not sufficiently marked to warrant the isolation of the mind in a realm all its own, sundered from nature. In reality, we know motion or life only in terms of mind. We agree to classify certain activities as "mental," others as "physical," but that does not mean that they have no interchangeable activities. Take away all motion, and you remove all basis of belief in a natural world; but you as surely rob mind.

In closing the present discussion, we must ernphasise the dual aspect of consciousness as thus far considered, (1) consciousness as brought in upon us; and (2) consciousness as emanating from within. The discovery of a world of activity, that is, the discovery through the fact of activity that there is a world, implies a corresponding or co-operative activity springing from the soul. In later chapters we shall make more use of this fact. Here we simply note its bearing on the preceding discussion, and chronicle the relationship of activity and consciousness as equally fundamental, although activity may antedate our consciousness of it. The soul, then, is an active as well as a conscious being. Activity is a phase of consciousness, and consciousness is a phase of activity. There is of course a difference between mere thought and thought in action, although all our thoughts, all our ideals tend to express themselves in action. But activity is always present in some form. The final statement about life must include both the forces of nature and the highest activities of the soul, the sentiments of love and beauty, the joys of our spiritual existence.

Our analysis of the nature of existence, therefore, has revealed two ineradicable factors, though we have not established the argument for activity on as firm a basis as that for consciousness.* (1) Existence is fundamentally conscious, and (2) existence is fundamentally active. A third characteristic has only been briefly referred to, namely, existence is also social. So far are we from being isolated or subjective beings, that life would be impossible were it not for our dependence on one another. The discovery of the self is a social discovery. We become aware that other beings are here before we know that we exist. The self is discovered by contrast with another self ministering unto us. From the first moment, we live in a social world and we can never get outside of it. There is every reason, therefore, for the development of a social rather than an individualistic system out of the fundamental facts of consciousness. All parts of life are inextricably bound together. The study of existence from the point of view of consciousness does not in any way impoverish our conception of life; it greatly enlarges it. Thus we return to the point of view of the universe of manifestation. In the profoundest sense we must understand the divine order, and the relationship of souls in that order, before we can truly evaluate either the phenomena of nature or the activities of mind.

*The question of activity will be considered in other chapters.

Chapter V
Mental Life

WE are now in possession of a general way of thinking about the objective and subjective realms of existence. The universe is a system of natural objects and mental beings individually made known to us through consciousness. Every thing, every individual is related through this universal system. The objective world seems to be composed of independent forms and hard substances. Yet all forms are transient. The dense material dissipates into invisible gases and chemical elements; and we find nothing permanent until we turn to the realm of the invisible and persistent Power which is revealed through these shifting forms. Even the constant qualities of matter must have their basis in a more substantial Reality in order to be constant at all. Matter is eternal only so far as it purposefully belongs to the universe which manifests this self-existent Reality. It is law-governed because that Reality is unchangeable, it has no meaning until we view it as part of the very consciousness, the objectified life of God Himself, of the God who is in His world, immanent in evolution and in the human soul.

The Reality revealed through the outer and inner worlds, then, is one. Everything exists by virtue of the presence of God; and we, existing in Him, contemplate and know His manifestations, in part. We do not simply feel matter as composed of distinct objects. We do not simply feel sensations of light, heat, and cold. An object, a blow, a sense of warmth, does not come directly to the soul. The object must be understood, the blow must be perceived and reported, the feeling of warmth must be translated into an idea. We feel, and also know that we feel, force or matter in some of its forms. The simple act of feeling and knowing implies the existence not only of an objective world from which our sensations come, but of a conscious being to whom that world is made known. These very words become intelligible to the reader only so far as they call up ideas; and back of these ideas, following one another in rapid succession in the reader's consciousness, is the reader himself contemplating, pondering these ideas, and associating them with whatever ideas reflective experience as already made clear.

Even the materialist, in affirming that matter alone exists, is stating a product of reason. He has put certain ideas together, and evolved them into a system. This system of ideas is absorbing.

It is his habitual mode of thought and colours his entire conscious experience. As a natural consequence, he neglects one aspect of that experience. He forgets the nature of ideas, affirms that mind is a mere "flame," a product or outgrowth of matter. But even in admitting this he surrenders the stronghold of materialism, since by his own admission this " flame" is conscious; and consciousness is the fundamental fact of existence. It involves all that we are, all that we know, desire, and feel, the whole universe, and the great Thinker himself.

An essential point in all this is the fact that a portion of everything that man sees, feels, hears, or in any way experiences is due to his understanding, from the moment his discriminating consciousness is quickened. The world becomes comprehensible to him as fast as he himself develops to comprehend it. Gradually his emotions and his knowledge play a greater and greater part in his life, until he develops a personal atmosphere, which projects itself into the objective world. Impulse and imagination sometimes give place to reason, but thought is no less influential, man is as truly leading a life of mind.

All this is so readily forgotten that it needs constant emphasis and repetition. Man forgets that he is a soul with a body, that he is primarily a conscious being, contemplating ideas and influenced by thought. Yet, consciously or unconsciously, some idea is always prominent with him. He is always devoted to something. He shapes and controls life by his thought. Yet, just because the influence of thought is constant and is a fact of the commonest experience, man is unmindful of its power, of the real nature of his life. He seems to be leading a material life, and accordingly permits himself to be overcome by that which is material. But even here it is belief that governs his conduct. As a conscious being, he could be governed by nothing less than consciousness. Every act of conduct is due to a direction of mind; and the mind shapes the conduct, draws to itself whatever corresponds to the desire or thought, as truly as a magnet attracts particles of iron. As this may not yet be fully evident, it is well to consider the influence of thought at some length; for in this neglected factor of human experience we shall find the greatest help in the problems of daily life.

The foregoing discussion was necessarily somewhat abstruse. But we now turn to a line of reasoning wherein the evidence is easier to follow. All that is needed to put the mind on the track of unlimited evidence is to give it an impetus in this direction. In the profoundest sense all our thinking, all our conduct, is regulated by our directions of mind; and what we most need in any case is a new perspective. We are ever seeking to break free from imprisoning directions of mind. When we have had a "spell," a fit of "the blues," we realise retrospectively that we "got into a wrong direction." All our objectionable states, all that we seek to be free from, belongs in part at least under this head. For although action must follow a changed direction, the chances are that when we have changed the direction of mind we shall modify our conduct. Your infatuated daughter or son whom you would set free, is in a "wrong direction." There are emotional states concerned, but if you persuade your child to look at the situation differently, the emotions will change. The dogmatic friend who will not reason will nevertheless respond to love, and with love will come a new vision. Thus we might pass the whole of life in review and everywhere find exemplifications of the same law.

The artificial methods of reasoning of which we have spoken are directions away from life; the solution, we found, was to turn back to life. And what is duality of self but the downward and upward directions whereby the same facts are viewed? The pessimistic attitude is the direction into, especially the direction into the flesh, down deep in sensation. All the world is changed when the vision is turned upwards. And so with the conclusions of the preceding chapter. When we have thought ourselves into the conscious world, we may turn and look out, not in any sense imprisoned. The point of view in a word is, to start with consciousness and then see all things in the foreground of that, within that. Our analysis is removing the scales from our eyes that we may see ourselves as we really are in the act of life, not as our materialistic opinions would make us out to be. In our thoughtless years we think we are free. When we begin to think we discover that instead of seeing things as they were we were really seeing only what the habitual state of mind made possible.

It is clear that the impression made upon us by a given experience depends largely upon the opinion we put into it. Let a company of people of varied tastes, prejudices, and education read a thoughtful book, listen to a speaker of decided opinions, or attend an entertainment of considerable merit, and their comments will display a wonderful variety of opinion. Diametrically opposed opinions on political, religious, and philosophical questions have been maintained ever since man began to reflect. A slight or a very marked divergence of opinion separates mankind into little groups and sects the world over. Each sect offers its opinions as truth. Everywhere people accept and are influenced by opinions with surprising readiness. Thousands of people have been made miserable and thrown into a state of excitement because in their fear and ignorance they accepted the teachings of dogmatic theology about sin and a future state, to say nothing of slavery to medical opinion and the untold suffering that has grown out of it. The credulity of human nature is one of its profoundest weaknesses; and I need only refer to it to suggest its bearing on our mental life. It is a guiding factor with the majority of people, and opens the door to the control of the weak by the clever, the strong, and the unprincipled. Every one is deceived at times through eagerness to believe rather than to understand, and the influence of prejudice is so subtle that only the keenest and most discerning minds are able to eliminate it to any marked degree.

We are so accustomed to obey certain ideas that we are scarcely aware of their power over us, or how true it is that "the world is what we make it." We are born with a set of ideas, born members of sects and parties in which theory, practice, and prejudice have become one. Our religion, education, and even our fears are prepared for us by other minds. Every opportunity is given us to develop in traditional directions, and it is deemed almost blasphemous to have ideas of our own. Even if in later life one is quickened in a new direction, it is almost impossible to overcome and cast aside these deeply rooted opinions and prejudices.

We seldom pause to question our beliefs. Prejudice will not permit it. People, as a rule, prefer to accept an opinion without attempting to prove or disprove it. They are bored—and it is a most lamentable fact—they are bored by reasons and proof. It seems never to have occurred to them that man is free, and sure of his own individuality and the truth, only so far as he has gone with a rational process of thought. The tendency to think for one's self—the sanest and most helpful tendency in man—is crushed out in its infancy; and our whole system of traditional religion tends to shape man's belief for him. It is only when some unusually original or self-reliant thinker breaks through the hard-and-fast lines of rut-bound thinking that any ideas of fundamental value are given to the world. The non-sectarian and unprejudiced man of science is a very late product of evolution; and even he is prejudiced against many religious doctrines, and as rigorously excludes all facts that lie without the boundaries of natural science as the most bigoted conservative rules out the doctrines of the radical. The love of truth is not yet strong enough to lead us to seek universal truth rather than particular opinion. We think we know. Preconception blinds our eyes on every hand. We give credit to this man or this sect, as though there could be a monopoly of truth, when a little reflection would show that truth is universal, and does not hold because any man enunciates it, because any sect champions it, but because it is implied in the nature of all things and persons.

It is a revelation to the majority of people to discover the power of fear in their lives. Fear enters into their religion. It is the basis of the prejudice which stifles inquiry. It enters into every detail of daily life. We are apprehensive, as a race. We picture calamities of every description, and dread the worst. The sensational press supplies constant material for fear. We fear to eat this and that. We dread, anticipate, put ourselves in the attitude to receive what we fear; and we live in constant fear of death. Fear is simply another form of opinion. It runs back to our willingness to believe rather than to think for ourselves.

But the one who knows the law and obeys it without fear, the scientific man or the seer, as truly as the savage, is in a sense erecting his own world from within. The world is as large, as intelligible as man's ability to interpret it. The artist discovers qualities in the outer world which actually do not exist for other people. He detects certain lights and shades, certain undulations of the landscape, and an endless variety of transformations during the four seasons of the year. A scientific man will discover evidences of glaciation, and read a long and most interesting history from a rock which may be a worthless obstacle to the farmer. Even the beautiful Alps were once deemed so many obstructions to travel before the love of natural scenery was developed. The same scene viewed by the novelist, the historian, the warrior, the man of business, the savage, presents so many different aspects, depending upon the training and the class of facts which serve the purpose of the observer. It may be comical, it may be tragical, it may inspire happiness, sorrow, comfort, dread, chagrin, pity, suggest a thousand different ideas to as many beholders. All these aspects may have some basis in fact, but they are not complete pictures of the outer world. They are individual phases of it. We see things as we are.

The difference, then, is deeper than education alone. There are natural tastes, likes and dislikes, affinities and sentiments, so that the saying "What is one man's meat is another's poison" is equally applicable to the inner world. Passion colours the world according to its nature and intensity. Experiences, dispositions, theories, differ, and project themselves into every fact of life. One thinker is persistently optimistic, despite all that life brings of pain and misery; another is no less strong in his pessimism; while a third is so bigoted that he cannot be induced to take a fair view of anything, not even of his own persistently biased nature.

The very fact that the world is so large, that the supreme Reality is known to us only in part, so far as experience has made it known, shows that our interpretations must differ, and that the difference is in us. Indeed, one may seriously question if the limitations of temperament will ever be overcome, if one man can ever describe life except as he sees it, modified by the general knowledge of the race. Perhaps that individuality is fundamental in the purpose of God. If so, it is each one's duty to cultivate this profoundest individuality, and discover what God means through it, what aspect of life one is best able to interpret. This deeper life in mind must then take the place of the superficial world of opinion. The dogmas and influences of other people must be rigorously excluded until, in moments of quiet reflection, one learns the divine meaning as revealed in the individual man.

Thus the individual thinker penetrates deeper and deeper in his analysis of our life in mind, until his consciousness seems to blend with the universal Thinker, of whose consciousness all life is purposefully a part. His means of knowing the objective world, and the influence of opinion, of prejudice, education, and temperament, prove to him that he lives in mind. But now he discovers a yet deeper reason, and once more happily makes his escape from tile narrowing effects of mere self-consciousness into the greater consciousness of relationship with the Universal.

The difference between one person and another, then, is fundamental. One has only to try to put one's self imaginatively into the mind of a friend in order to realise this great difference. Let the friend be one's closest companion, one's brother or mother, whom one has known intimately from infancy; and even here the transition is impossible. There is something that we cannot grasp, because it is the friend's experience, and can never be ours. Personality—what is it, whence came it, and what does it mean? Your world and my world, how much alike, yet how dissimilar! How many and varied the aspects of a single personality as presented to different people, all equally true perhaps, all drawn out from a single source under ever-changing conditions! Self exists within self-the social self, the self of impulse and emotion, and the self of reason, the conscious self and the subconscious—wherein we view ideas in all their aspects until they become fixed habits of thought—the fleeting ephemeral self, which reveals itself in an endless variety of moods, opinions, and feelings, and the permanent self which we call "soul"—that deeper consciousness which is intimately related to the Supreme Self.

But some aspect of self is always uppermost. To this we are for the moment devoted, and it is this more superficial self or direction of mind that we are most concerned with in this chapter. On the one hand come impressions from the world of matter. On the other come thoughts and influences in the sphere of mind. The two unite in consciousness, and form the world of mental life, our interpretation of the great whole of which we are parts. In the centre exists man. Looking one way, all that he sees is apparently material. Looking in the other, all appears to be mind. When he seeks their unity, he finds it alone in the conscious self which underlies both of these mental directions.

Another aspect of our mental life is well brought out by an article entitled "The Personal Equation in Human Truth,'" by Reuben Post Halleck, who points out that "our own actions do not raise in us the same feelings as similar actions on the part of others. Egoistic emotion is more or less present with all. Egoistic emotion invariably warps the truth. We do a thing, and it seems all right; another does the same thing, and it seems all wrong. A man of high moral ideal found fault with his neighbour for working on Sunday about a suburban house, The following Sunday men came from the city with a view to purchasing some lots which the moral man was desirous of selling. He took the prospective buyers over the lots with great alacrity, showing the good points. The neighbour reproved the moral man, who became extremely angry. Labourers frequently denounce a trust with great bitterness of feeling, and yet they proceed to form a labour trust with the express purpose of making labour dear and shutting off competition. They refuse to let an outside workman mine coal, except at the risk of his life, although his children may be starving. Do the workmen experience the same feeling of indignation at their own conduct in forming a trust as they do toward other trusts? A woman was one day genuinely indignant because candidates lacking a certain characteristic had been elected members of her club. In less than a week she was trying to secure the admission of a friend who lacked precisely the same quality. No feeling of indignation at her own conduct ruffled that woman's brow this time. We frequently hear it said, 'If I were to do as she is doing, how angry she would be!' There is one test which the majority of persons can apply to themselves. They have told another something in confidence, and have felt indignant because he betrayed that confidence. There are very few persons who have not at some one time in their life betrayed a confidential secret to someone else. Amusing as it seems, it is common to hear a person accuse himself of a breach of trust, saying, as he tells a secret, 'This was told me in confidence.' His egoistic emotion will not allow him to say, 'I am not worthy of confidence,' although he would unhesitatingly draw that conclusion in the case of another. . . .

"It is confidently remarked that the egoistic emotions cannot warp mathematical truths, for they are inflexible and unerring. Such a statement might do very well in schoolrooms, but it has no place elsewhere. A noted lawyer said: 'I have a client who is a plaintiff in a damage suit. Now, a damage, if expressed at all, must be mathematically expressed. My client's damages amount to the sum of two and two, or four. But he cannot possibly add his own two and two of damage without making the sum five. The defendant adds this some two and two and makes the sum three. If it were not for the fact that the emotions of self will not allow men to add units correctly, quite a percentage of my practice would be gone. If men were sure that selfish emotion would not prompt another man to take advantage of them when opportunity offered, a still larger percentage of my practice would be lost.'

"The undoubted fact that our own acts do not cause in us the same emotions as similar acts on the part of others is one of the strangest psychological truths. This legacy from unevolved man, from the times when brute might was the only right, has been handed down to us. This legacy is still a beam of varying size in every human eye. We shall probably long continue to excuse certain acts of our own and of our friends and to criticise our enemies severely for those same deeds. We see this tendency full-fledged in animals. A big, strong dog will take away a bone from a starving dog. A wealthy railroad president and wealthy directors will plan to wreck a rival road whose bonds and stock may constitute a large proportion of the investments of some orphans. These men would experience intense emotion if anyone attempted to steal from a child of theirs. They will steal from the children of others without a qualm. The advance in intelligence has many times served to increase this tendency. Napoleon was a very intelligent man. The promoters of hydra-headed trusts are men of great sagacity. It is nevertheless true that, as a man acquires the habit of reflecting on his own actions, as he by an effort places himself in a neutral position, and from that changed point of view looks at his deeds with another's eyes, as he puts himself in the place of those whom his acts have inconvenienced or wronged, this brute legacy, so destructive of truth, will grow less and less. But only the possessor of a vivid imagination, either natural or acquired, can ever succeed in doing this. Children who are early taught to regard each act from the point of view of those affected by that act are placed in the royal road to overcome this tendency. A successful businessman recently said that he did not wish his children thus taught, for such training would put them at a disadvantage in the struggle for existence.

"True conceptions are hampered not only by those emotions which are popularly termed peculiarly egoistic, but by all emotion, which a searching investigation shows to rest upon a hidden foundation sunk deep in those feelings which affect the self for weal or woe. All emotion has a twofold aspect in regard to thought and the search for truth. On the one hand, emotion supplies all the interest we feel in any subject, and is thus absolutely necessary for all long continued, earnest thought; on the other hand, there is thus a deflecting power necessarily at work in the centre of every thought. The strong desire to prove a certain theory has led the most honest of men to look at certain facts through coloured glasses. it is often dangerous to consult any medical specialist at first, because he will have a tendency to see unmistakable signs of the complaint which he treats."

But aside from these subtle deflective tendencies there are many other aspects of our mental life. To consider them is no doubt to enter the realm of the abnormal, the mystical and the doubtful, yet no account of the inner life is complete without at least a suggestion of the part they play. Recent investigations have shown that the study of hypnotism throws much light on the nature of mind. The mind is even more susceptible to hypnotic suggestion than to opinion. Opinion itself often comes in the form of suggestion, and brings hypnotic influence with it. The so-called magnetism that accompanies the spoken word is often more effective than a strong argument. Thus the strong-minded sway the weak; positive leaders draw negative minds about them and new dogmas are forced into fashion. As knowledge of the power of suggestion grows the dangers are greater. Hypnotism itself becomes a cult, in due course, and all kinds of occultism, spiritism, and the like, follow hard upon the new cult. The only resource for those who would know the truth that is well-nigh lost in this mystical confusion is to undertake an investigation as thorough as that of F. W. H. Myers.

It is plain that the conscious self shades gradually into the great realm of the subconscious or "subliminal." It is no less plain that the saner moments of human life shade gradually into nonsense. A Myers or a James is able to see the truth and state the law; for the majority there is no dividing line between the spiritually sweet and the psychically unsound.

Without specifically inquiring into the phenomena of telepathy, the influence of mind on mind, and of mind on body, it suffices for our present purposes to note that these experiences point to a more intimate relationship than we have suspected. There are far more influences at work in the inner life than any single science or theory takes into account. Our theories lead us to draw sharp lines of demarcation where in actual life there is gradual transition. The popular way of regarding the relationship of mind and matter, namely, as shading off imperceptibly into each other, is in marked contrast, for example, with the view of mind-matter relationship which originated with Descartes. According to the latter view, mind and matter are as sharply contrasted as possible. Each constitutes a little world by itself, the one being purely conscious, the other entirely automatic and mechanical. The theory that mind and matter are parallel, but do not interact, has developed from the days of Descartes until it has become the general scientific way of regarding the question. On the other hand, there are eminent psychologists who still believe in the causal efficacy of consciousness. For example, see the chapter on the "Automaton Theory" by Professor James in the most human treatise on psychology in our literature.* The question is too large to engage us here. The reader is free to reject the foregoing suggestions in regard to the close relationship of mind and body and yet be ready to follow the general trend of the chapter, the purpose of which is to show the unsuspected depth and richness of our life in mind. Whatever the nature of the hazy experiences in the vague outskirts of our normal consciousness, these vague experiences at least play their part in the inner life, and must be taken account of in the present discussion.

*Psychology, vol. I., chap. v.

Now that psychology has become one of the natural sciences and is concerned with the mental states which are found in closest correspondence with bodily conditions, there is all the more reason for free inquiry into the inner life. The most profitable hypothesis for the practical investigator is undoubtedly the popular belief that mind and body interact. It is by putting one's powers of activity to the test that one most readily learns what theories are unsound, what doctrines are true. To undertake such experiments is to be convinced that there are many more lines of activity and spheres of mental influence than psychology now takes into account. It may not be necessary to investigate the alleged facts of the "pseudo-sciences," the various "planes" of which theosophy speaks, or delve into the mysteries of spiritism. But the psychology of the beliefs in such mysterious realms is at least of consequence. A complete science of the inner life would at least complete the circle of psychic influences, and put up sign-boards, as it were, on the borderlands of the occult: "Here theosophy begins." "That way the Hindu Yogi practices develop." " Over yonder are kept the spirits of the mighty dead, ever ready to be summoned." "This path leads to adeptship, that to mediumship."

The topography of the inner world thus established, one might at last be able to distinguish the normal from the abnormal. There would be nothing more to fear in the inner world. For knowledge is power, and to see through a mental state is to master it. It might still be true that there are valuable facts to be learned by excusions into the occult. But the question would be, Is the venture worthwhile? People who are profoundly in earnest to help humanity, or who are deeply in love with the religious life, are pretty sure to answer emphatically, No! The best that one brings home from such excursions is a certain acquaintance with the inceptive stages of occultism by the aid of which one is put in a position to warn other people when they are on dangerous ground. There are so many people in these days who have been misled to think that there are hidden powers of great consequence which one may acquire by occult practice, that one needs to utter such warnings very frequently. It is safe to say that there is no "hidden wisdom" which has been secretly handed down through the ages that can for a moment be compared with an ounce of common-sense.

The inner life is not mysterious. The mental powers we are all of us using, out in the broad daylight, as it were, are the greatest and the sanest. It is a question of using these powers more wisely. If there are also subconscious or subliminal activities which may be brought more and more into consciousness and into control, then let this extension of influence grow out of the sanity of common-sense living. One may well wait for sane-minded explorers to develop these resources before engaging to depart very far from the usual round of intellectual activities and earnest Christian living.

The psychologist who, with rigid logic, excludes from his investigations all mental states except those which are parallel with brain phenomena, is not of course in the right attitude to discover whether there are any "higher" mental powers or not. He is a specialist, and his particular field is well worth cultivating. Meanwhile, the man whose life has room for the mentally spontaneous may well become a specialist of another type. His task is to discover what may be wisely accomplished by voluntary mental action. Hence the question of mental influence upon bodily states is for him of prime importance.

Yet oftentimes the discovery of the bondage of mind to matter is of far greater import than the fact of mental influence on bodily condition. Many a man is set free from what he called "himself," or from what he took to be genuine "spiritual" feeling, by learning that he was harbouring a pathologic condition. We are warned by Professor James not to judge by pathologic conditions but by values, outcomes, results. But it still remains true that a physio-logical state is oftentimes mistaken for a "spiritual" condition. No field of investigation promises to be more fruitful than the sphere of mental bondages to physiological conditions. Already, people are beginning to conclude that crime is oftentimes the mechanical result of diseased bodily condition. Possibly our whole treatment of criminality, and of insanity, too, is on a wrong basis. When we begin to realise how little power the mind has under the conditions of brain life into which the majority are born, we may begin to get some light on the cause and prevention of crime. The average man is a creature of impulses and physical passions. The age of self-control has scarcely begun to dawn, and the age of reason—well, that is very far ahead. *

*The reader is advised to supplement this and the two following chapters by the study of a treatise on psychology such as vol. 1. of Professor William James's "Principles of Psychology;" "Psychology, Briefer Course," by the same author, or, "Outlines of Psychology," by Professor Josiah Royce.

Chapter VI
The Meaning of Idealism

—

FROM the present point of view, the first value of the inner life is experience as individually interpreted. Instead of running hither and yon in search of wisdom and power, one should learn that the centre of wisdom and power is within. Instead of rushing from deed to deed, one is to reflect, philosophise about life while it passes. And instead of merely thinking about life, one should enter into the spirit of it, realise the power and beauty of the present moment.

Since the realisational aspect of our inquiry is of paramount value, one should take time to reflect sufficiently upon the considerations which are at present engaging us to become accustomed to the idealistic method of thinking. The value of discussions such as the preceding chapters briefly suggest is that one is enabled reflectively to make the transition from the world of appearances to the realm of reality, to think one's self into a position whence one may look forth upon the universe as veritably a whole. Then one thus idealistically enters into the fulness of the present, experience will be seen in an entirely different light. The old sense of mystery will be gone, and with it the old pessimism, the sense of antagonism and duality. For one will possess a principle of unity in one's own life, and a unitary principle by which to interpret experience. The significance of the principle will not be seen at first. It is necessary to repeat the process of reflective transition many times before one is really at home in the world which the idealistic analysis reveals. But the essential is the point at which the mind arrives, the way life looks when one is able to pause on the idealistic summit and look about.

There are a number of misconceptions that arise whenever the idealistic theory of the universe is proposed. These misconceptions we have already noted in part. But it is necessary to indicate them more specifically, since very much depends upon the inferences that are drawn from idealistic premises. To declare that the universe is known only through mind has been supposed, for example, to mean that there is no matter. Hence a direct appeal to matter in some of its most tangibly real forms has been deemed a sufficient refutation of the entire theory. Elsewhere I have pointed out the absurdity of this notion so far as the idealism of Bishop Berkeley is concerned,* and I have also shown that many systems of idealism that are said to be purely speculative have a thoroughly practical value. But it is important to consider other aspects of the subject since it is only by extreme persistence that one is able to avoid all misconception.

*See "Man and the Divine Order," chap. xiii

To declare that the world is made known by its presence to the mind is of course very different from the assertion that the world is existent only in the mind. What is present in the mind is an exceedingly elusive flux of ever-changing states. One cannot even know one's self except by analytically and synthetically passing beyond the merely given stream of consciousness. If the world of nature is at last fairly well known by means of ideas it is not until these ideas have been evolved into a system. The mere sense of acquaintance with the world counts for very little. Everybody is in process of wresting from the world its meaning by the aid of ideas. To grasp the truth of idealism is in the first place simply to attain a knowledge of facts. A man scarcely begins to know what a fact is until he learns that he is an idealist. It is not argument that makes a man an idealist. We are all idealists now. To awaken to the fact is by no means to lose anything. The world of nature is not proved one whit less real by the discovery that for man it has no existence apart from conscious experience. The qualities that have been discerned in matter, as distinguished from mind, are as distinct as before. There is as good reason for the continuance of scientific investigation according to the experimental and laboratory methods. There is even more reason for the pursuit of universal truth, regarded as of value in itself, apart from individual caprice, whim, prejudice, personal preference, and the like. Not one single point is lost for the world of reality. Man is granted no license. He is no less subject to law. Life still lies before him. The essential difference is that a fundamental error has been corrected. The illusions which once beset experience have been so far swept away, the dualism so far overcome, that it is now possible to regard the universe as grounded in invisible reality, in Spirit, the clue to which is found, not in the senses, but in the domain of thought, of insight. Therefore, when the transition has been made, and one is able to look upon the world from the idealistic point of view, one is ready at last to face life in earnest. For a man is obviously at great disadvantage if he regards himself as a mere being of flesh and blood.

If man asks, What of it? when you have shown him how to think himself free from sense-life, point out to him that everything depends on it, that he is now in a position for the first time to understand what reality is. Formerly the question, What is real? would have seemed absurd; for apparently all that one needed to do was to open one's eyes to see things as they were. Now. it is clear that only by taking thought may one ever learn what is real. The discovery once made, it is surprising what a wealth of considerations immediately confirm it.

It is a truism to declare that our senses deceive us, or rather that we draw false inferences in regard to our sensations. Life intelligibly begins for us when we learn to reason correctly in regard to our sensations. In addition, there are all the illusions of feeling to overcome, the deflective power of the beliefs in which we are reared, the influence of prejudice, emotion, fear, and all the varied mental states which we have considered in the preceding chapter. It is plain that we have actually projected our mental life into nature, whereas we seemed to be victims of the world. If things possessed us, it was after all the thought of things, it was our theory concerning their place and reality. The materialist is in a sense as much of an idealist as any one else, the chief difference being that his consciousness is less enlightened. Things are pursued as of worth in themselves merely because we fail to see their true nature. Materialism is accepted as a philosophy only by those who are ignorant of the nature of the sense perceptions on which their theories are reared. Generally speaking, man is so far a prisoner of ideas that it requires much wrestling with the facts of experience to make this discovery. From infancy to old age, man is making his life in accordance with ideas—in so far as he has any power over it. To become a conscious idealist does not mean the acquisition of new and entirely different power. No man could ask for more or greater power than he is using or misusing moment by moment, and day by day. It is not a question of changing from power to power. By making the transition above described one does not in reality lift the mind over the barrier from the world of things to the world of ideas. There is no such barrier. One is already present where all ideas and all powers are. It is primarily a question of consciousness, of substituting good philosophy for bad theory.

An important cause of our trouble, then, is our beliefs. We have accepted ready-made convictions instead of reasoning for ourselves. Hence we have put ourselves at the mercy of creeds and dogmas. We have not seen life as it is; we have regarded it with the eyes of opinion. We have not pursued what was real; we have gone in quest of illusions, simply because others had gone in pursuit of them. We have not lived for ourselves; we have worried through the wearisome days, in bondage to beliefs which we thoughtlessly accepted. Thus we have unwittingly created out own happiness and misery. Nobody has really enslaved us, no one could put unconquerable bonds on the soul. But we have permitted ourselves to be the victims of ideas without even asking if life might be otherwise.

The resource is perfectly plain. It would be foolish to spend a moment in regret. For it is precisely by way of such experience that we advance to mastery. Life precedes thought. Only by first having experience do we possess aught to think about. And now, lo, and behold! we have been acquiring through all these years of bondage precisely the machinery needed to make ourselves true conquerors. We need not go forth in pursuit of power. All power is resident here. We need not even ask, Where is God? We have lived and thought with the Father all the way along. From first to last we have been sons of God, living in heaven, using angelic power. But we have not known it—that was all. Now we know it. Now we see through the glass clearly. Never could God be found without, if He were not first discovered within. No truth could be true unless its winner proved it. Not all the angels in heaven could put a man in possession of the knowledge and power which is thus gained. In the very nature of the case, truth must be wrestled for. Only by living and possessing life for one's self is it ever life. And the life's the thing. The moment that is just now passing is the real moment, and this moment is real to the one who apprehends it. Your moment cannot be my moment. Mine can never be yours. Life is eternally an individual possession. How clear is the way, how true that each must do and know and triumph for himself!

Yet, as surely as the idealistic discovery leaves the world of nature as real as it found it, so surely does man continue to be a social being. Only through mutual aid do we make any progress in the effort to understand the world. Service is as much a law in the rational world as in the realm of society at large. Although there is a discovery which each man must make, and a changed attitude that is individually imperative, nevertheless only through the aid of others is man able to make the advance. Idealism leaves him precisely what he was before—until he voluntarily profits by his great discovery. And if idealism reveals any fact at all it is that we are related each to each with far greater intimacy than we had ever, as realists or materialists, suspected.

Again, we are left as we were as active beings. Described in simplest terms, man is a reactive individual in the presence of an environment. It is impossible to feel sensation and remain still. Life pulsates, changes, accomplishes. Moved upon by life, man must be up and doing. Idealism shows him how he has been acting all along. Every belief tends to express itself in conduct. To accept an idea is to be inclined to live by it. Hence if we would alter our conduct we must change our beliefs. It is false theories that lead to our trouble. We have reacted upon impulse without question. We have accepted the judgment of others without asking if it was righteous. Then we have vainly tried to free ourselves from the results by working upon the effect. But the only remedy for error is truth.

Finally, the idealistic discovery leaves man as wilful or selfish as it found him. Sometimes idealism has been understood to be the rearing of a man's own mental world from within,* hence the new precept has been: Build any world you like. Now one may indeed construct any mental world one chooses. One of the greatest services of idealism is the revelation it makes in regard to the mental worlds which people project into nature. There is nothing in the fact itself that prevents a man from continuing in this course. The questions, What is ideal? What ought I to do? are quite different from the mere matter of fact. Hence the great issue is this: What sort of world ought I to build from within? What is real? What is worthwhile?

For example, see lecture on "The Romantic School," in "The Spirit of Modern Philosophy," by Prof. J. Royce, Houghton, Mifflin & Co., 1892.

No conclusion could be more false than the supposition that the world is what I make it by my thought, therefore I can make it what I will. To assert, to affirm the self, to make "claims" and demands, as if the universe could be shaped by one's will, is to create illusion upon illusion, to be in a worse plight than the materialist. It is precisely because of these self-assertions that reality has been hidden from us. The true conclusion, the moral of the idealistic tale, is entirely different. If you would know what the world really is, you must obey Christ's injunction and rise above your mere self. For the true world is the realm of the universal. The particular interferes with the universal until it is thoroughly understood and constant allowance is made. The Christian precept is at one with the precept of Greek philosophy and of modern science. Only by allowing for the personal equation may one make headway. The universal is indeed made known through the particular. But, the particular must first be seen in right relations. It is the point of view of the whole that explains the part. Only by looking around and beyond the particular fact may we truly apprehend it.

Hence the importance of a sound theory of first principles is clear. The same principle that guides us in the pursuit of truth is the starting-point in the world of conduct. The individual must make a certain discovery and adopt a certain attitude. But this is only the beginning. The fruits will show whether he has really found the universal.

It is safe to say that more false conclusions have been drawn from the discovery that life is fundamentally an affair of consciousness than from almost any other metaphysical statement. The illusions are far more subtle in the inner world. The errors of mysticism, pantheism, and idealism are far greater than the errors of materialism. The very discovery which should set man free is made the vehicle of fresh bondage, new dogmatism, and greater selfishness. In truth, there is ten times the reason why one should avoid the deceptions of the inner sense, the pronouncements of unscrutinised intuition. It requires no great insight to avoid the illusions of our physical senses; the test comes when we try to discriminate between emotion, preference, caprice, impulse, and unscrutinised intuition, on the one hand; and the "higher" promptings on the other. Here, indeed, the empirical method is the only one—the individual experiment tested. by reason. The discoveries of Idealistic philosophy do not afford the slightest excuse either for indolence, or for selfishness. Life is as much a problem as before. There is the same need of experience. But there is less excuse for our sin. Say what we will about inheritance and environment, we now see that our own attitude is the most important factor.

Experience is an evolution in the presence of ideas. It means much or little to us according to the degree of insight into the part played by ideas. But the part played by ideas is in a sense secondary to the resulting conduct. Hence, to arrive at the great discovery is to see the need of fresh examination of the nature of the will and the resulting conduct. It by no means follows that a man may become free by simply sitting down to think. The demand for action is hard upon him. And the important point is that the way to truth now proves to be up the hill of righteousness. Thus the results of philosophical idealism are so different from what has been supposed that the inquirer may indeed rub his eyes in wonderment. A thousand false theories are refuted in a moment by the great discovery. It hardly seems necessary to single them out. Suffice it that one has arrived and all is changed. Arrived, did we say? Yes, at a point where we may at last begin to live—but life is ahead.

So many people deviate when they discover the power of thought that we must be sure to see what follows, and avoid putting too much emphasis upon it. Only by constant repetition of a few great truths, regarded in many lights, may we hope to avoid the pitfalls of false inference. It is one thing to arrive at a conclusion and another to act upon it. Our beliefs do indeed tend to become "rules for action," but there is no necessary connection between theory and practice. Many a thought is ephemeral. Scarcely one idea in a thousand is made significant by the actions that are shaped by it. We could slay ourselves a hundred times a day, if thought sufficed. Fortunate is it that the majority of our thoughts have so little power. Strictly speaking, thought in itself has almost no power; it is what we do in the presence of it that is of consequence.

It hardly seems necessary to dwell on the difference between theory and conduct, so clear is it that mere thought is by itself entirely ineffective. Everyone knows people who hold theories that have no connection with their practice. From one point of view that is the chief fault to be found with people. Speculatively inclined people invent doctrines which they would never dream of applying. Others have a set of beliefs to live by and another to preach about. It is not strange, then, that some have said, A man's real belief is revealed by what he does, not by what his lips confess. Were men compelled to put all their beliefs to the empirical test there would be an unprecedented revolution in human thinking. Moreover, a great many a priori doctrines would be entirely upset. There is profound truth in the saying that "seeing's believing." To see is often to be utterly amazed and to confess that one's prejudices were entirely unfounded. Nothing brings more surprises than real experience.

There is clearly a difference, then, between ideas about experience, and ideas that withstand the test of experience. There is great difference between thinking about a course of action and actually making the effort to carry it into execution. Again, there is a difference between mere thought, desire, will, and the ideas that we are actually able to carry out in this great universe of law and order. Finally, there is an important distinction to be drawn between our theories about the world, and the activities of consciousness which make the world known to us—despite all theories and volitions.

All through the idealistic ages too much stress has been put upon thought. Hence idealism has led to fine-spun theory rather than to conduct. Hence the misunderstandings that have arisen when idealism has been mentioned. But ordinary idealism is only a starting-point. It clears away a certain misconception in regard to substance and power. The way once clear, the question arises, What is power, and to what end? What am I, the thinker, in essence? To affirm that "I think, therefore I am," is to say very little. To declare that the world is understood through thought is not to explain the world. The world is also misunderstood through thought. Whether or not the thought be true is a question which thought cannot answer without the aid of experience.

Let us put the statement "all is mind" to the test by asking if this proposition is exhaustive. Is the term "mind" comprehensive enough to include all that modern science tells us about matter? What is matter, as nearly as we can distinguish it from mind? In simple terms, it is describable as tangible, hard or soft, liquid or gaseous. It possesses certain exact chemical qualities such that two parts of hydrogen, for example, unite with one of oxygen to produce water. By placing the water in a certain atmospheric condition it may be frozen; by applying heat, the congealed water may be turned into a fluid again. This fluid may again be reduced to hydrogen and oxygen, by means of an electric current, and both of these gases may be ignited. In all these various forms, solid, liquid, gaseous, combustible, the same particles persist in differing relations.

What meaning have any of these terms if applied to mind? Mind is describable as intelligence, awareness of sensation, volition. You cannot saw or chop an idea, nor can you weigh an aspiration. Mind does not occupy space; in a word, its characteristics are in many respects decidedly different from the qualities of matter. You may, for example, stand before a burning building, wishing that you could stop the work of destruction. You have a vivid consciousness of what is taking place before you, but the mental state is very different from the chemical change popularly known as "fire." To stop the fire, you must apply certain liquids in large quantities. If you do not discriminate, you may increase the work of destruction; for example, by throwing a keg of powder on the flames.

"But this is a very absurd case," the advocate of the " all-is-mind" theory exclaims. " Of course powder will cause an explosion. But what a person puts into the body produces an effect in accordance with his thought about it, or at least the subconscious thought of the race about it." No, I reply, the case is not extreme. If "all is mind," as the advocate of therapeutic suggestion uses the term, powder is as mental as food. If, however, powder possesses qualities of its own, we may with equal truth declare that substances put into the body contain powers which act independently of human thought. The fact that bread pills, for example, when given to a hypnotised subject with the suggestion that they are a powerful drug, produce the effects of a drug, is another affair. That the mind influences the body is unquestionable, but that neither proves that matter is without inherent qualities, nor that matter is mind; it simply proves the greater power of mind. Even if man could put out fire by "holding a thought," that would be no evidence that fire is mental. To prove that one thing is more powerful than another is not to prove that they are identical. That the world of matter is known to man only through mind does not then imply that this world is merely an "apocalypse" within the human mind. Obviously, matter did not come into existence with the first human being; the data of natural science are too exact to permit such a belief. Evidently this earth existed many millions of years prior to the appearance of man. Its qualities are therefore pre-human. In other words, they exist independently of the mind of man.

"But they exist in the mind of God," our opponent declares. In what way? As thoughts in our minds exist for us? That would hardly account for the persistent substantiality of the earth, the spatial grandeurs of the starry heavens, the vivid reality of the great cosmic fire, the benefits of whose heat we daily enjoy. Evidently God's universe is more real than the mental hypothesis implies. Moreover, if we assume that mind and matter are identical in the mind of God, we surrender all the distinctions which we have found essential to a correct understanding of either mind or matter. Both mind and matter may be grounded in the activities of Spirit, but that is very different from the statement, "all is mind"; for if we regard matter as a mode of manifestation of Spirit, we find the basis of it in the larger spiritual life of the universe, the basis both of nature and of human consciousness. Its law is then divine, spiritual, not mental; I must understand and adjust myself to its law; I ought to study the great world of nature as the embodiment of God; a very different attitude from that suggested by the statement, "all is mind."

If it were true that "all is mind," there would be no limitations to thought, mind would be at liberty to make its own laws, which is what the advocates of this doctrine really counsel. To think that one possessed five dollars would be the same as to possess them, to think one's self ill would be equivalent to being ill, and to affirm health would be at once to have it. An endless number of fallacies follow, the moment this proposition is accepted. On the other hand, if we conclude that we are conscious beings living in a psycho-physical world, we ask, What are the laws and the lessons of our twofold existence? If our life is both mental and physical, it is obvious that both matter and mind are limited, organic. The mind affects the body, and the body affects the mind. We are dependent upon matter not only for all immediate acquaintance with the physical universe, but we are compelled to use it as our vehicle of expression—except in cases of telepathy, and even that may be due to wave-motion in the ether. On the other hand, the great glory of existence here is that we may transcend the physical while still living in it, in dependence upon it. The wise man neither forgets that he is living a life of mind, with laws of its own; nor that he is living a fleshly life, with laws which are no less stringent. He strives to live above physical sensation, so far as matter is burdensome; and to conquer the temptations of the flesh by the power of mind. But he does not try to use thought when he ought to use food or sunlight. Thus he recognises the beauty of all things in their place, and regards both matter and mind as revelations of the love and wisdom of God.

Another important point in regard to the significance of idealism is its application to the theory of knowledge. The subject is much too technical to engage us here to any extent, but a brief reference is necessary in order to guard against agnostic conclusions. For centuries the discovery that all our knowledge comes by way of perception and ideas has led certain philosophers to conclude that therefore human knowledge is hopelessly limited. It is but one step farther to the conclusion that man knows only his own feelings and thoughts. Hence the famous and oft-quoted saying of Protagoras, "Man is the measure of all things." That is, each man knows his own perceptions simply, he is limited to the appearances of things when, and as, those appearances arise. Man cannot then know what is true and right. He is shut into the world of his own relativities.

One might argue in the same way in regard to the religious consciousness and therefore reject the belief that God is immanently knowable. Many have argued in this way and have concluded that God is simply man's belief. This would reduce God to a mere ideal, as changeable as human ideals in general. The conclusion would seem to be substantiated by the historical evidence that man's God has changed as rapidly as his beliefs have changed.

No doubt there is a profound truth in this discovery of human limitation and relativity. Every thoughtful person must face the hard facts sooner or later. The discovery means the rejection of many theological doctrines as anthropomorphic. But there is a far more profound discovery than that. For evidently there are two points of view from which human relativity may be regarded. One may either conclude that owing to man's limitations he is forever shut off from knowledge of reality. Or one may conclude that relativity, relationship, is precisely the condition through which such knowledge is obtainable.

In regard to communion with God, for example, it is clear that there are two factors to be considered. There is both the human uplook and receptivity, and the divine spirit. Christian theology of the Augustinian type has been inclined to put the emphasis on the divine "grace"; it is not by man's own efforts that he is "saved, not because of his own worthiness; but it is the divine "election." Hence, all that the worshipful soul could do was to contemplate the divine glory. Later thinkers have come to the conclusion that the Father rewards all men according to merit, that human activity plays its part, According to this view, there is both the proceeding forth of the Spirit, and the individual attitude of approach or rejection. Hence the experience is co-operative, relational. Only by taking account of both factors may one be true to the Father-son relationship.

If we pause to consider the nature and scope of human experience, we discover that there is not a single experience that is not relational. Consciousness means precisely consciousness of something by something, it is nextness, awareness through presence. Since we possess experience in no other form, there is no reason to talk about knowledge or reality in any other form. Were we deprived of the relationship we should be excluded from the reality. All experience is co-operative, all knowledge is knowledge of co-operative relations. We may consider now this factor of the relationship, and now that. But there is no reason for the conclusion that we are excluded from knowledge of the one half simply because we know it relationally.

As important, then, as it is to discover that we know the world through consciousness, as many allowances as we must make for the forms and modes of human cognition, the important fact is still the world-order, whose system, law, reality, our wills have in no wise created. When the last word has been said in regard to human thought and the neat, cosy little worlds it can build for itself, the only consideration of much consequence is the nature of things, the real system whose magnitude utterly dwarfs man with his puerile schemes. It is well to ascend a mountain and look forth upon the world, or gaze into the starry heavens and try to conceive of the extent of the solar system. Then, by contrast, one may look back upon the subjective idealist imprisoned in a little world of his own making and be thankful that one has escaped.

Retrospectively, one sees that the relativity of consciousness is simply one among many facts which characterise the nature of things. The nature of things viewed as universally as possible is the great consideration. Nature is not intelligible alone.

Human consciousness is not intelligible by itself. There are no "things-in-themselves." There are no minds by themselves. We must break away from the notion that a "thing" can be handled or known apart from the handling and the knowing of it. We must lift ourselves out of the subjective slough and stand upon the heights of universality, The universe in this larger sense is intelligible only from the point of view of its ultimate Ground. The Divine Order is the real nature of things. In that Order nature is but one of the domains. In that Order all souls are grounded. It is too high to be "seen." It is too far to be "felt." It is not in any sense an object of perception, nor even of intuition. The mere understanding can scarce attain to an acquaintance with its unity, for the understanding becomes involved in contradictions, antinomies. But reason, the highest faculty in the human soul, can indeed attain knowledge of the supreme system, for that system is the Universal Order of Reason, and human reason is by no means separated from it.*

*For a more exact and historical account of idealism, see "The Spirit of Modern Philosophy," and "The World and the Individual," by Professor Josiah Royce. A. C. Fraser's "Selections from Berkeley," Clarendon Press, Oxford, is an admirable introduction to idealistic philosophy.

Chapter VII
The Nature of the Mind

—

WE have now made the reflective transition from the outer world to the inner. Generally speaking, we have seen that the world is made known to consciousness. This does not mean that the world is unreal, or that it is like our thoughts. For we have found it as necessary as before to distinguish between the permanent and the transient, the world of desire and the world of law and order. It does mean that the universe is of the nature of mind or spirit, in some ultimate sense of the word, but the ultimate reality is obviously far more substantial than our ordinary thinking and far more real than our will. We are all members of a world-system and consciousness is the means whereby the presence of that system is made known. Through our ideas we endeavour to understand experience. But there is a vast difference between the reality that is ultimately the same for all, and the theories which differ so widely among individuals. Furthermore, there is within the general world of consciousness—which may be said to be more or less alike for all—an inner world of great variability, the world of whims, moods, and opinions, some aspects of which we considered in Chapter V.

Having reflectively made the transition to the centre of mental life, we have found that all conscious experience is co-operative. We are not isolated individuals. We do not know of the experience of the simplest perception apart from that which is in a sense the not-self. Perception relates the mind to the world of nature. Through the exercise of will we also learn that life is a co-operative experience. It is only our wildest fancies that are to any degree removed from the world of reality. To attempt to carry out a plan of action is to discover that at best the realisation of will must be matter of adjustment. The mental act known as volition involves a sense of effort, and through this effort we learn that we are immediately environed by powers that exist quite independently of our wills. It is through activity rather than through thought that we come into rough and convincing contact with the world. Hence, in the preceding chapter we have found it necessary sharply to distinguish between the qualities which our activity-experiences reveal and the realm of mere thought, caprice, mood.

As long ago as Buddha's time it was said that "all that we are is the result of what we have thought; it is founded on our thoughts, it is made up of our thoughts." In the Maitrayana Upanishad, also, it is said that " thoughts cause the round of a new birth and a new death. . . . What a man thinks that he is; this is the old secret." Modern devotees of the same doctrine are fond of quoting the Old Testament passage which states that "as a man thinketh in his heart so is he." We have seen how profoundly true this is in so far as man's opinion of himself is concerned. But it is no less clear that it is not what we have thought that has made us what we are; it is what we have done. In the first place, if we had really taken thought our conduct would have been profoundly different; for most of our regrettable actions were impulsive. And in the second place, there is a vast difference between thinking and doing. Buddhism itself is really founded on this fact, for in the long run it is said to be our accumulated actions, that is, our "karma," that make or unmake us. Our accumulated actions are said to affect us in the next "incarnation" even though memory fails to hold over. In other theories of man's inner life the emphasis is put also upon action instead of on thought. No law is more dreadful for some people to contemplate than the law of action and reaction. From our thoughts there is indeed escape, but when we have once acted the die of fate is cast. The only remedy for a bad action is a good one.

The real test of a theory of human experience, therefore, is its relation to the world of action. It makes all the difference in the world what we agree to call the power, life, or force which experience makes known to us. If we deem it "physical," we are likely to become materialists. If we denominate it "spiritual," the outlook upon life is vastly changed. If we cower helplessly before it we become fatalists. If we vainly think we can do with it what we will—we learn the lessons of bitter experience. To call it "love" is to adore. To beat against it, instead of wisely seeking to learn its laws, is to become a pessimist. One of the strangest conclusions at which man ever arrived is expressed in the condemnation of pain as "evil." Pain, as we shall more clearly see in the following chapter, is due to the ill-adjustment of some part of the bodily organism which nature is seeking to remedy. To meet pain with resistance is to increase it. Hence we see of what vast import it is to arrive at sound conclusions in regard to the powers that play upon us.

In the first place, it is a question of sound psychology. Each man may perform the experiment for himself and learn to distinguish thought from action. To think one's self into the centre of mental life is to find the mind surrounded by activities. That is a hard-and-fast fact of the greatest significance. The fundamental character of activity clearly recognised, the practical problem is this, Granted all these activities, how may I most wisely adjust myself to them? What kind of thoughts are superficial, and what thoughts are followed by action? Obviously, it is the thoughts that we enter into dynamically that affect our conduct; all others are as fruitless as the theory of a speculative metaphysician who invents his own world-scheme. The important point to consider, therefore, is not the thought as such, but what we do with it and how we react upon it.

Having sufficiently emphasised the fundamental importance of activity, in so far as we are now concerned with it, we may well give attention to the law that is exemplified in the preceding inquiries into our mental life.

If we observe a little child at play, we notice that it turns from this sport to that, from one plaything to another, as rapidly as its attention is attracted. The first indication of definite growth in the baby's mind is this concentration of its baby eyes and its blossoming consciousness on some attractive object. The observant mother early learns to govern the child largely through its interested and skilfully directed attention. A little later she discovers that it is far better both for the present and the permanent good of the child never to call it "naughty," and thereby call more attention to its unruliness, but to interest it in some new play, or carefully and persistently to point out the better way, until it shall have become absorbing.

The student absorbed in his book so that he is oblivious of the conversation going on about him illustrates the same power of a fixed direction of mind. The performance of skilled labour consists largely in the cultivation and concentration of the attention, together with the necessary manual accompaniments. The art of remembering well depends largely on the attention one gives to a speaker or book. That speaker or book is interesting which wins and holds our attention. That thought or event influences us which makes an impression, and becomes part of our mental life through the attention. We learn a language, grasp a profound philosophy, or experience the beneficial effect of elevating thought, rid ourselves of morbid, unhealthy, or dispiriting states of mind with their bodily accompaniments, in proportion as we dwell on some ideal or keep before us a fixed purpose, until by persistent effort the goal is won.

What is hypnotism if not an induced direction of mind suggested by the hypnotist? When the subject is under control, and hypnotised, for example, to see a picture on the wall where there is none, the whole mind of the subject is absorbed in seeing the supposed picture, and there is no time or power to detect the deception. Many self-hypnotised people are equally at the mercy of some idea which is the pure invention of their fears. Insanity best of all illustrates the nature of a direction of mind pure and simple, with the wonderful physical strength which sometimes accompanies the domination of a single idea. All strongly opinionated people, those whom we call "cranks," the narrow-minded, the creed-bound, the strongly superstitious, illustrate the same principle, and from one point of view are insane—insane so far as they allow a fixed state of mind to control their lives and draw the stream of intelligence into a single channel; whereas the wisely rounded-out character, the true philosopher, is one who, while understanding that conduct is moulded by thought, never allows himself to dwell too long on one object.

The point for emphasis, then, is this, namely, that in every experience possible to a human being the direction of mind is the important factor. In health, in disease, in business, in play, in religion, education, art, science, in all that has been suggested in the foregoing, the principle is the same. The directing of the mind, the fixing of the attention or will, lies at the basis of all conduct. The motive, the intent, the impulse or emotion, gives shape to the entire life; for conscious man is always devoted to something. Let the reader analyse any act whatever, and he will prove this beyond all question.

The whole process, the law that, as our direction of mind so is our conduct, seems wonderfully simple when we stop to consider it. Yet we are basely conscious of the great power we exercise every moment of life. We are not aware that, in the fact that the mind can fully attend to but one object at a time, lies the explanation of a vast amount of trouble, and that by the same process in which we make our trouble we may overcome it.

Yet we know from experience that painful sensations increase when we dwell on them, and that we recover most rapidly when we are ill if we live above and out of our trouble. On the other hand, we know that a wise direction of mind persisted in, or the pursuit of an ideal without becoming insanely attached to it and impatient to realise it, marks a successful career. Without the generally hopeful attitudes of mind embodied by our best churches, and expressed in our beliefs about the world, we should hardly know how to live in a universe where there is so much that is beyond our ken.

We are ever choosing and rejecting certain ideas and lines of conduct to the exclusion of certain others, and into our choice is thrown all that constitutes us men and women. The present attitude of the reader is such a direction of mind; and this book, like the world at large, means as much or as little as the reader is large and wise in experience. In the same way this book, or any other, reveals the life and limitations of its author. It cannot transcend them, it cannot conceal them; for in some way, through the written or spoken word or through mental atmosphere, personality ever makes itself known. The world is for us, and for the time being, "what we make it," because only so much of it is revealed as we can grasp. In whatever direction we turn our mental searchlight, those objects on which it falls are thrown into sudden prominence for the time. The world is dark and full of gloom only so long as we dwell upon its darkest aspects, and do not look beyond them. There are endless sources of trouble about us. On the other hand, there are innumerable reasons to be glad if we will look at them. We may enter into trouble, complaint, worriment; we may make ourselves and our friends miserable, so that we never enjoy the weather or anything else. Or we may be kind, charitable, forgiving, contented, ever on the alert to turn from unpleasant thoughts, and thereby live in a larger and happier world. The choice is ours. If we fear, we open ourselves to all sorts of fancies, which correspond to our thought, and cause them to take shape. If we communicate our fears to friends, their thought helps ours. If we become angry, jealous, or act impetuously, we suffer in proportion to our action. If we pause to reflect, to wait a moment in silence, until we are sure of our duty, we experience the benefit of quiet meditation.

It is the explanation of our actual situation in this well-ordered world, dwelling near the heart of the divine Father, that sets us free, and makes us masters of our conduct. It should not therefore be a new source of terror to learn that we are beset by all sorts of subtle influences, or to be told that thought-directions are instrumental in causing misery and trouble. These wrong influences cannot touch us if we understand them. Our whole being is a protection against them, if we have reached a higher plane. There must be a point of contact in order for one mind to affect another, some channel left open, just as there must be an affinity in order for two persons to form a friendship. Our safety, our strength, lies in knowing our weakness, in discovering that the law of direction of mind is fundamental in every moment of human life. If we continue in the same old way, complaining, fearing, thinking along narrow lines, and submissively accepting the teaching of others, it will not be because we do not see the law.

Out of the mass of impressions and opinions which for the majority of people constitute mental life, we may eliminate those that bring harm, and develop those that are helpful. The economy of cultivating right thoughts is thus at once apparent. Matter is obviously as much of a weight and a prison as we make it by our habitual thought. Looking one way, we enter into matter, or density. Looking in the other, we invite that which is spiritual, quickening. Ideas have power over us in proportion as we dwell on them. It is matter of real economy, then, to view ourselves and our habitual ideas from as many directions as possible, precisely as one goes away from home in order to break out of the ruts into which one inevitably falls by living constantly in one atmosphere.

Man leads a life of mind, then, because he is a conscious being, because the stream of consciousness is turned now into this channel, now into that, and can only take cognisance of a relatively large aspect of the world by the broadest, least prejudiced, and most open-minded turning from one phase of it to another. He has a distinct individuality, for which he is personally responsible, which it is his duty to preserve and to develop. It is through this, if he thinks for himself, that the keenest light is cast upon things; for it is the fundamental direction of consciousness, and is ultimately related with the Self who knows all directions. Next in order comes daily experience, shaped by education, inherited beliefs and tendencies, and whatever leads the mind into a given channel. After these fixed directions of mind come the mere fleeting influences, mental pictures, fears, atmospheres, perplexities, and troubles, which affect the mind superficially, yet possess a tendency to strike deeper into the being, become fixed habits through subconscious mental activity. The law is everywhere the same, namely, that the conscious direction of mind, supported by the whole personality, is controlling for the time, since the mind can fully attend to but one object at once. Its application to daily life is at once apparent.

The next point to observe is that the idea which wins our attention and upon which we react is not alone effective in the immediate present but is productive of subconscious after-effects. Here again we see the importance of distinguishing between mere thought and thought that is followed by action. The power which thought seems to possess comes from the activity which the attention directs. A thought is more or less influential to the degree that active attention is given to it. It is action and reaction that are equal, not thought and reaction. The attention directs the activity and the subconsciousness responds. It is sufficient for the actively conscious state to establish the direction; it remains for the resulting activity to carry out the decision.*

For further aspects of attention see Stout, "Analytic Psychology," i, 189. Stout carefully distinguishes mental attention from its physiological accompaniments. Hence it is made clearer that we are able to direct attention from within.

Consequently, few discoveries are of greater practical value than the disclosure of the law of subconscious mental activity. For this apparently limitless realm below the threshold of our voluntary life exemplifies in unsurpassed degree nature's law of least resistance. That which we labour and groan to achieve consciously, comes easily and directly in the subconscious world. There friction is at its minimum. There a thousand deflecting tendencies of our personal life are out of the way. There our souls undoubtedly lie close to God from whom power and wisdom come in ways that are only limited by our conscious ability to assimilate and understand the result. For always there is help in the subconscious world. Never do we turn to it in vain.

We mistake if we think that it is the idea or experience which we try to coerce into our selfhood which becomes most truly our own. It is more apt to be an idea of whose power we were but slightly conscious when it dawned upon the mind, but which struck deep into the heart and was brooded upon for weeks and months. After such a period of mental evolution is over we can indeed trace it to a vitalising idea found in a book, heard from a philosopher, or beheld in an intuitive flash. But when it thus struck home we were little aware to what it would lead. Crucial experiences of many kinds are only understood in perspective. We know what people were worth to us when they are gone. We know how deeply we lived when the emotions were touched, when we parted from old associations and began a new career. Our profoundest conclusions are gradually acquired subconscious possessions, inductions from long experience, which one day rose into the region of consciousness. We do not fully know what we believe until a new experience calls scattered notes into a theme or unifies detached themes into a symphony. The music we hear in our most conscious moments is only a note or two out of a great harmony. We live in scattered bars, phrases, and movements, except in those occasional hours when an entire harmony sounds from below, or when the walls are parted and we hear the great oratorio from outside and the celestial hymns from the beyond.

Life is in the profoundest sense rhythmical, a constant waving, a rising and falling over the crests and down into the trough of the sea. If our conscious vision were larger we should look from crest to crest, and behold the harmony of our long evolution. When we descend we should know that it is but to rise. But, absorbed in sensation and self, not even our memory lasts over, until repeated philosophising has made clear the law. It is safe to say that every one of our doubts, fears, and complaints is due to this lack of perspective or memory; yes, that all our suffering is maladjustment to the wave which is carrying us ever forward, forward, whether we are adjusted or not. Our subconscious life is of particular assistance in the solution of the problems of suffering and evil, since it is the convictions which we develop by subconscious induction that finally make clear the law.

Those whose instruments are most intimately attuned to the universal harmony of things agree in the description of it as rhythmical. The heart beats rhythmically, the breath comes in rhythms, every function of the body proceeds in rhythmic sequence. The seasons come and go, the stars fade and re-appear rhythmically, the entire universe is as truly a pulsing harmony as when the angels sang at the creation (which never began).

The poets and musicians feel this universal rhythm and reproduce it in verse and concords of sweet sounds. In them there are fewer conscious and subconscious obstacles. The same harmony exists for all, but owing to mal-adjustment we feel and therefore report it as discord. You will observe that the less a man possesses of that quality which we call the "soul-life" the more prosaic he is. Let a man pursue the pathways of the Spirit, and he will gradually become more refined in voice, manner, language, thought, and feeling. This refinement bespeaks a closer relationship with the rhythm of things. His language becomes more rhythmical.

If we could view the subconscious process we should doubtless find greater receptivity to the inmost vibrations of the universe. We should then see why Julia Ward Howe could rise in the night and write her Battle Hymn of the Republic with scarcely any thought of what she was writing—as it came fresh from the rhythms of the subconscious world. We should know why many spiritually illumined people have written hymns. Perhaps we should learn that the priestesses at the famous Greek oracles gave forth their utterances in hexameter because there was a rhythmical psychic experience of which the utterances were the expression.

We may then be justified in describing the divine spiritual involution itself in terms of rhythm. This may be the ultimate basis of what we call evolution. The different natural forces may be varying rhythms of the one life. The vision of things under the aspect of eternity, or as one whole, would then be an intuition of the great rhythmic play over the great ocean of life whose billows, seen from below, are moments of time.

But no argument is needed in these days to show that there is a relatively boundless subconscious world. The experiments of the French scientists, the splendid work of F. W. H. Myers, the reports of the Society for Psychical Research, and the contributions of writers on suggestive therapeutics, have made us familiar with an endless array of evidences. The question is, granted that there is a subconscious mind, how may we make use of its powers? In the answer to this question we shall develop in this chapter the outline principles of a theory of spiritual psychology, which will serve us in various ways to the end of the present inquiry.

It has been evident from the start that the psychology implied in our discussions is thoroughly practical. It has been evident too that we have widely departed from contemporary physiological psychology. In this chapter we shall follow the same clue, and omit all discussion of side issues as not germane to the present plan. Professor Munsterberg admits that for questions of value, worth, and the ultimate character of psychological states, we must look outside of physiological psychology. And here we are confessedly dealing with values and meanings. We are determined to master our own minds as clues to the worth and reality of life. Our psychology is therefore a part of our general philosophy. We shall do well, then, to regard the mind as an evolution exemplifying a purpose. That is, we may most profitably study it as the realm of realisation of ideals, always active subconsciously and never pausing in its flux during our waking hours.

Professor James thus states the case: "The pursuance of future ends and the choice of means for their attainment are the mark and criterion of the presence of mentality." The stream of thought ever flows forward, it is always changing, and it always tends to be part of a personal consciousness. As the stream flows, the act of attention is the most striking characteristic, the selection of one thought from the stream which when chosen thereby becomes to some extent an end of action. "My experience is what I agree to attend to." "Only those items which I notice shape my mind—without selective interest experience is an utter chaos." Thus the essence of your mental life is largely will, your consciousness is teleological. Martineau defines will as "the act of choice which settles an alternative." You are hesitating between two courses of action and now at last you decide. The decision is equivalent to pressing a button which sets machinery free. Or, better, the act of will gives a teleological or purposive tendency to the subconscious mind. The volitional tendency thus becomes an embryonic course of action; and the subconscious mind is exceedingly fertile soil for its development. Moreover, it is very discriminative. For it has many functions to perform. Now it is told to awaken you at six o'clock tomorrow morning, and now an ideal is committed to it which you may realise in a year or more. Now it is a minor decision, and now regeneration of character. First you consign to it a mere hint, and then you expect it to assimilate a whole book. But press it as you may it apparently is never weary. The subconscious mind is at least as large, as versatile, and as well trained as the entire series of moods which constitute one's mental life. Therefore if you would increase your subconscious power begin by training your conscious mind. As much system as you consciously possess you will surely have given back to you. If your conscious self is vague, dreamy, you may expect vague and incoherent subconscious revelations. Your mind grows by what it feeds on; therefore select your mental pabulum. Selection largely depends upon desire. Desires depend upon their choice by will.* Will depends upon attention, or issues in the act of attention. The power of voluntary attention depends upon the degree of self-control, which in turn depends upon the degree of composure and of self-knowledge. Therefore if you would strike at the heart of purposive or evolutionary mental states, begin by acquiring peace, poise, equanimity, as the basis of wise attention.

Note also the close connection between feeling and will. Wundt paints out that "without the excitations which feeling furnishes we should never will anything. Feeling, therefore, pre-supposes will, and will feeling."

All this seems simple and clear enough when one's attention is called to it. But are we not apt to say, "This shall be so"; to exert our wills, forget the higher Power, strain after ideals, claim that which is not yet true and can only progressively become so? Do we not dwell in thought somewhere way off in the clouds or in the distant future, instead of wisely adjusting ourselves to the immediately advancing present? Is the will really so powerful that it can abolish time? What is the will, and what is the nature of its power?

When I raise my arm and move my hand, the various motions which I make seem to be controlled by my will. Yet I know very little about that apparently simple process. The hand and arm are moved by certain muscles, the muscles by a certain nervous discharge, which obeys definite laws utterly beyond the power of my will to control. I simply desire my hand to move in a particular way; and, lo! a wonderful mechanism, perfected by nature long ago, is set into activity. The complex motions by which I move my arm and hand are matters of habit rather than of will, and I use nature's mechanism almost unconsciously. The whole body responds to my thought in the same manner, and the great outside world goes on almost regardless of my will.

What, then, is my will? Has it no power? Assuredly. But its power is seen in the inceptive stage of our most subjective activity. The will-act follows upon the selection of alternatives. When reflection has settled upon this course of conduct in preference to that, the fiat is issued, and the resulting action follows upon the sense of effort. Only the reflective and volitional stages are conscious. When the mind has assumed a certain dynamic attitude, the subconscious mechanism accomplishes the result. Hence, to modify or change conduct one must begin by thinking more wisely. To think is, as we have repeatedly noted, by no means to act. Yet it is what we believe, what we accept, that we act upon.

The first determinant, then, is the direction of mind; the second is the dynamic attitude. The will consists in part of conscious attention, and in part of activity or volition. The act of attention is the direction of mind. The volitional effort sets the machinery in motion. Hence it is in one sense true to say, with Professor James, "that what holds attention determines action." The child ceases his play, and turns his whole activity in some new direction because his attention has been attracted. We thread our way among the obstructions of a busy thoroughfare because our thought is fixed on some distant object. The hypnotist shapes the conduct of his subject when he has gained control of the subject's attention.

Will is a direction of mental activity with a definite object in view. It is the conscious side of conduct, and as such it wields great power. Will uses power. It gives definite shape to power. It opens the mind to power, so that "I will" is equivalent to " I am ready." A man with a strong will is one who persistently keeps a desired object in view. The human power lies in the desire, the natural in that which fulfils it. Here is a very important distinction. By longing for an object we unconsciously put ourselves in an attitude to attain it. We move towards it. We exclude everything else in our efforts to attain it.

Again and again we forget that will gives shape to directive power, and act as though it were a force which we must exert. But my will alone is powerless to move my arm. I will to move it, and at the same time co-operate with nature's mechanism and my own well-established habits. If I kept saying, "I will move it," "Now I will move it," it would remain motionless. By saying, "I will do this," " I will have things thus and so," one is apt to produce a nervous strain, to assert our own power, as though the human will were omnipotent. Self-conceit and ignorance of the larger and diviner life accompany such self-assertion, and close the door to the higher power. The Spirit quietly withdraws at the approach of such assertion.

It is important, therefore, to note that it is not necessarily the most conscious exertion of activity that is most effective.* Absorbed attention, a fixed direction of mind, is itself an act of will. To concentrate upon an idea is to draw power to it. On the other hand, to become free from an undesirable emotion or idea one should not combat it. Do not then try to suppress it or push it out of your mind by an exertion of will; persistently turn your attention to another mental object, each time your thought drifts back into the old channel. Thus you will gradually undermine the old habit and transfer its energy elsewhere. The principle is the same as the law of use and disuse in organic evolution. A function grows with use and falls away if disused. An idea grows if attention is paid to it. To rid your mind of an idea turn vigorously from it to another.

For an account of the various stages of consciousness and self-consciousness as related to the more ethical aspects of mental life, see Professor Palmer's admirable little book, "The Nature of Goodness," Houghton, Mifflin & Co., 1903.

In other words, it is a matter of habit. To establish a habit you must launch your energies vigorously and persistently enough in the new direction to overcome the resistance offered by your organism. That is, set up motion in that direction. An object once in motion tends to continue in motion unless impeded by some obstacle or counter motion. In this case the obstacles are most likely to be other habits, your conservatism and accustomed beliefs. To be opinionated, dogmatic, bigoted, is to offer an unyielding front to new ideas. Once win the interested attention of a dogmatic person and you may instil that subtle softening influence which shall melt away the barriers and set the soul free. Our inner life, both mental and cerebral, is a mass of such habits or tendencies; and the art of inner evolution consists largely in the wise adoption of flank movements, or methods of outwitting our unruly and therefore unyielding selves. Professor James advises us to "launch ourselves with as strong and decided an initiative as possible." We thus arouse vigorous activity in the newly chosen direction.

Note then that to transfer your attention to another set of associations, another group of mental pictures or way of thinking, is to establish a new centre of equilibrium. This means that down through your mental life, including the subconscious, there is a response, a new motion which tends to become a habit. A change of creed or philosophy, a change of heart and of associates, a love affair and a disappointment, are illustrations of marked alterations of equilibrium. But these marked changes are typical of results that are constantly occurring in a small way, whenever we become absorbed in ideas. The same principle which makes us victims of our moods thus becomes our servant when we understand this law of mental equilibrium and the art of attention which is the clue to it. We have greater power over our motor ideas than we have suspected. The difficulty has been that we did not set about character building in the right way. Generally speaking, we find what we look for. Our lives are shaped by what we desire and will to desire. If we would control the after result, we must then start at the centre—by wiser choice between alternatives, keener discrimination, more thoughtfulness, more patience, and withal more trust in our subconscious minds.

If you would know how to further your mental evolution, learn the laws by direct study of your own mind. Thus you learn what you desire by observing yourself in the act of desiring. You learn what you are by what you do. There is no single experience or intuition which tells you what you are; it is by gradual discovery that you become acquainted with your true meaning. The unity of the self, the central will is deep-lying, so deep that it is sometimes hard to believe there is a unity or central purpose. For we know ourselves largely as fragments, as subject and object, inner and outer, conservative yet wasteful, selfish yet unselfish, centripetal and centrifugal. A deep unity is implied, however, in all this in congruity. Every day and hour there is unity amidst all this variety; and this profound relationship is typical of the great One amidst the Many which we call God and His universe.

Just because the unity holds all the variety, it is too great for us to grasp in a single moment. Hence we should not expect to know the full self except progressively. It is not a mere unity on the subjective side, any more than it is an objective or observed unity. The self is both the subject that contemplates and the objective mood, thought, feeling, or action contemplated. What you are in deepest truth is the unity of these moods and you are the moods too. Do not think of yourself, therefore, as merely the observer. You are all these high desires and aspirations. The self that is just now acting, is your soul, in part. The deeper self which attains a receptivity of which you are now consciously incapable is a function of your soul, living on continuously even while you are asleep at night. Do not then expect any miraculous intuition to tell you what you are. You are in part all that you think, and will, and act. If you cannot now realise yourself fully, when you will to be noble and true and great, it is only because the time has not yet come, there is not yet the proper correspondence between inner and outer, the soul and its environment. You must await the occasion.

Most of the problems in our psychological life are due to the sundering of that which is not separated in actual existence. Look within, and if you look truly you will note that every moment your mental life is an evolution. Every moment you are feeling, thinking, willing, and doing. These are not separate parts of your life, they are more or less distinguishable phases of an interchanging whole.* Now you are more conscious of yourself as desiring to realise a great ideal, and now you are painfully toiling in the valley to attain the great height. But you are no less truly your ideal self. You have not lost your hold. Your will is no less strong. The same soul is now seen in the toils of action rather than in the quietude of contemplation. But activity does not cease when you contemplate, and when you act you are still a resident of that eternal realm whose peace knows no waning. You can not think without in a measure being active. You cannot think without willing, that is, paying attention, when you attend you act, and when you act you think. You seem to be mentally disjointed only because the apex of consciousness is so small that you cannot pay attention to your whole self at once. But in reality what you discover in successive moments you are all the way along.

*The term "will," for example, refers to the whole meaning of our conscious life. See Royce, "Outlines of Psychology," p, 334 et seq. Professor Royce's treatise contains many practical suggestions of great value. For example, see his account of inhibition and self-control, pp.70-80. "What, in any situation, we are restrained from doing is as important to us as what we do.... 'Self-control' is an essential part of health.... You teach a man to control or to restrain himself so soon as you teach him what to do in a positive sense. Healthy activity includes self-restraint, or inhibition, as one of its elements. You in vain teach, then, self-control, unless you teach much more than self-control."

Chapter VIII
The Meaning of Suffering

—

IT was evident from the outset of our inquiry into the nature of existence that we were considering a system, an organised whole whose parts are apprehended by means of their immanent connections. Events in that system are found to move forward with a certain rhythm or regularity, describable in terms of law. Everything is related to everything else, cause leads to cause, and everywhere it is the point of view of the whole that promises to explain this inter-relatedness. It is difficult to see how a universe could exist unless its substances and forces were unified in an ultimate, orderly whole. A chaotic, an evil, that is, a self-destructive universe is clearly an impossibility. A universe must be good, must realise a unitary end, in order to exist. It takes nothing from the reality and worth of such a system to discover that it is apprehended and understood by means of ideas. As matter of fact, idealism puts one in a position for the first time to understand the real unity of the world. It is clear that there is one ultimate type of reality, that all the elements of life, however diverse in appearance, are grounded in one Self, whose nature is the basis of all law.

For the moment, it seems difficult to find a place for individual man in such a system. Everything appears to be determined by an all-embracing world-plan. Long before man awakens to self-consciousness, fate seems to have chosen for him. Inheritance compels him to suffer for the sins of his parents. He is born into a world of misery from which he vainly endeavours to escape. Life is at best a conflict. It does not apparently relieve the situation to be assured that, after all, experience is of the nature of mind. For one learns of the existence of a thousand unexpected bondages.

Yet this is scarcely one half of the truth. Man is indeed born into a well-established environment. Law everywhere reigns, and the world resistlessly makes itself known in a certain manner. But the mere description of experience is by no means an adequate account of it. The great question is, What is the worth of life? To what end? What are the ideals towards which the immanent Life is tending?

Man seems to be a product of environment. His thoughts and feelings are apparently the ephemeral outgrowths of matter. But, state the case as strongly as we may, we must add that man is also a reactive being. What he believes about life, what he does in the presence of environment, is of more consequence for him than the environment. The meanest facts are transfigured by the moral worth of a righteous deed. The mere fact that two or more alternatives are open before man, that as a moral being possessing the power of choice man may act for better or for worse, is alone sufficient to put the whole sphere of experience in a different light.

Life does indeed forever move forward. Man is compelled to live and to act. But it is only the most servile creature of habit who obeys instinct alone. In so far as man takes thought he practically makes of life what he will. If he humbly bows before what he is pleased to call "fate," it is on his own responsibility, it is because he has concluded that "fate" is unconquerable. The same principle or fact is regarded as fateful, or as an opportunity for the exercise of freedom, according to our belief concerning it. Once more, then, it is sound philosophy that sets man free.

It is clearly of the utmost importance to arrive at a rational conclusion in regard to the purpose of life, for in the last analysis our actions are regulated, not by the sum total of acquired tendencies and the play of circumstance, but by what we believe. Our conclusion may be rational or irrational, but for better or for worse it is made the basis of action. We may or may not formulate a satisfactory ideal. But be it dogmatic or tentative, we stake our chances upon it. In the absence of determining considerations, it is obviously rational once more to employ the empirical method.* Although we may not see the ultimate goal of the divine activity, we at least perceive certain definite immanent tendencies. Tentatively we may put before the mind the relative ideal which the facts suggest, then test that ideal by the actual results of conduct. For all practical purposes this is enough.

That is, one should take the clues of individual experience as guides. Life means to each of us what we make out of it.

Naturally, people differ very widely in the values which they assign to experience. Suffering means much or little to us according to the degree of actual benefit we have been able to derive from it. It may mean nothing at all, if our theory of life is constituted of borrowed opinions about pain and evil. It would be absurd to insist that suffering has the same value for all. The mere use of the term "progress," as applied to the facts of suffering, is confessedly the acceptance of an optimistic ideal. To indulge in such language is by no means to deny the pain, or to overlook the physiological aspects of it. But when all this has been admitted, when one has assigned the mental and physical facts to their proper spheres, it still remains true that there are entirely different ways of regarding the facts. From the point of view of the facts, alone, there are many considerations that indicate the evolutionary value of suffering. Whatever one's philosophy, then, there is reason to make certain primary distinctions.

In the first place, there is the actual activity denominated "pain." In the second place, there is the probable purpose or tendency of the pain. Finally, there is the sufferer's active attitude towards the powers that are displayed. Whether this attitude is one of resistance, of co-operation, or of resignation, depends upon the theory of pain held by the sufferer. Obviously, if one believes that the immanent tendencies of nature make for the good, the sound, and healthy, the active attitude will be profoundly affected by the conclusion.

Since it is a question of understanding and adjustment rather than a question of egoistic "affirmation," the problem is, What is the true principle of adjustment? The clue is already before us. We have found that life is not only fundamentally mental but that activity is common to both the mental and the physical worlds. We have seen that there is no chasm between mind and matter. We may study life from the point of view of activity and yet be on both sides of the "line" which is said to exist between them. What we mean by our descriptions of nature is that certain activities or vibrations are translated into what we call "consciousness." I do not see yonder patch of greens and browns, for example, as a motionless, dead thing. Certain wave motions are brought to my eyes, where they are translated into what we call "colour." I do not hear your voice as a thing by itself. My ears receive the vibrations, and my mind perceives the psychological result. Examine each of your experiences in the world of nature and you will find that they are made known to you through the mental correspondence to what is called "vibration." We are compelled to distinguish between mind and matter because there is a vast difference between (1) activities which, like the perception of fire, are involuntarily brought in upon us, and (2) those activities which, like an emotion, respond to the will. Your whole physical life is a mass of vibrations brought in upon you, reporting themselves in consciousness. When something interferes with the normal vibration, you are made painfully aware of the fact, and you naturally ask how you shall adjust yourself to the change. The whole practical question is, Is it possible not merely to "hold thoughts," but actually to bring about changes in the disturbed activities of the body? Obviously we must face this larger question, not confine ourselves to the mere thought, for it is the thought which is followed by action that interests us.

Having, then, reached the conclusion that the truth lies deeper than the plane of mental influences, though including these, let us look at the problem from another point of view. Let us regard the soul as a centre of activity, a centre of forces which play upon it. Consciousness makes us aware of the play of force. The vibrations are not necessarily mental; they are mentally known. The soul is acted upon, it is conscious, and it reacts—here are the essential points. We need not ask what these forces are, that is, how far mental, how far physical; but call them in general activities of Spirit. We may well leave to scientific scholars the adjustment of the differences of opinion existing between the regular physician and the mental healer. Our present task is far simpler, namely, the discovery of a doctrine which shall take account of the successes of mental healers yet avoid their excesses and supplement the half-truth in their philosophy. Let us venture the proposition that disease is disturbed action, that is, disturbed equilibrium, using that term in the most general sense. It need not concern us now how far the physical state conditions the mind, or whether the bodily state be largely subject to the mind. The disturbed action in question may either deprive the mind of its poise, or rob the body of its equilibrium; for it is both mental and physical. We are not now concerned to draw a line between bodily and mental influences. Suffice it that mind and body have evolved together, that they are always interrelated, and that in general anything which affects the one affects the other.

In a state of health every organ in the body functions rhythmically. For example, the regular beating of the heart, or the measured pulsations of the breath. Disease is a more or less general, temporary, or permanent disturbance of this rhythmic functioning. As surely as the heart tends to regain its normal action when the cause of temporarily increased pulsations is removed, so does every function in the body tend to recover its rhythm. This natural restorative instinct is the wisest provision in the entire physiological economy. Without it we should be powerless to survive. Pain is an indication that this rhythm has been disturbed at some point, that the forces are gathering to meet the injury and overcome it. It is nature's wonderfully beneficent warning that equilibrium has been lost and that we must obey certain conditions while the injury is being healed.

On the mental side the state which corresponds to this normal functioning is equanimity. Equanimity is of course somewhat disturbed when bodily equilibrium is affected, and the body responds to the mental state when emotions or other psychical activities mar the even flow of consciousness. Mind and body are like delicately poised instruments; either one responds to changed activity in the other. As here used, we understand by the term "mind," all temporary and habitual states of consciousness, such as sensation, emotion, volition, intellection. By the term "soul," we understand the spiritual being within and behind these states of consciousness and modes of activity.

In reference to disease, the disturbed action in question makes itself known to the soul. The pain translates itself into consciousness and calls for a reaction favourable to the recovery of equilibrium. From the present point of view it matters not so much what the particular pain is as the kind of reaction it meets at the outset. For the first warning sensation usually presents alternatives. In many instances the entire history of the disease depends upon the manner in which the inceptive disturbance is met.

Let us repeat, the soul is a centre of forces upon which it reacts and which it may learn to transcend and control. On the outside are the physical forces. Nearer the centre are the mental, and nearer yet the intimately spiritual. The heart of life is a centre of power and the kind of life found upon the surface depends upon the degree of spiritual consciousness attained. A man may be so absorbed in the physical life that he thinks himself a physical being. He may be so conscious of mental influences that he deems life a play of thought. Or, he may be spiritually so quickened that the mental life seems a superficial sport and play.

In case of illness, germs of contagious disease may or may not play a part. The state of mind or belief may or may not be favourable. There is something deeper than either germs or beliefs. It is not now a question of superficial factors. It is a question of the soul and the powers it uses. Suppose a person rushes to me with the news of a terrible railroad accident in which a dear friend of mine was probably killed. At once there is an uprush of emotions tending to disturb the equilibrium of mind and body. If I give assent, note this, if I give assent, such a reaction will surely follow. But, if I chance to be a wise man with a certain degree of composure, I recollect that such reports are apt to be hoaxes; and even if this one be true my friend may not be injured, or may not have taken that train. At any rate, I will await confirmation of the report. If it be confirmed in general, I will await particulars concerning my friend. If at last I learn that my friend was indeed killed I will meet the occasion with composure. To give way to excitement would avail nothing, and if grief comes it shall be more wisely expressed. Thus my mind passes through a number of inhibitions, or checks, until I decide what course to pursue. The success with which I each time take the wiser alternative will depend upon the habitual degree of repose, poise. Note, then, that behind the temptation to fly off my centre and give assent to the tendency to excitement, behind all my reasoning, there is a certain attitude of soul. The mind may affect the body, and may even control it; (within limits); but farther back is the soul which controls the mind. Unless my decision to be calm is supported by a well-trained soul, the mere thought may have little influence. The attitude of soul is indeed an acquired attitude, but it was acquired by facing situations like the above where actual force must triumph over force, where a greater must conquer a lesser.

Suppose now that the condition is a serious bodily state. The regular functioning or rhythmic action in the body is so far disturbed that the condition is known as "disease." The disturbed action or disease is due to overwork, a nervous collapse, or some other psycho-physical excess. Whether the first cause was mental or physical need not now concern us. The question is, How shall this disturbed action be met? By a superior kind of action which tends gradually to restore equilibrium.

Here is a woman, for example, who is a nervous wreck after years of extremely active life in the social world of a surging American city. For years, every hour of her life has been filled with intense, high-strung activity. There has been no time of true rest. There has been no complete recreation or change. All her capital has been spent. The last atom of reserve power was called into service long before the nervous collapse. Conventionally speaking, the woman has "nervous prostration," and that is all that is usually said. The wise doctor of medicine would frankly admit that medicine would be practically useless; it would only be given in case the patient's faith required it. He would say that the nervous organism must gradually be rebuilt during months and months of rest in a favourable environment. The nerves must be "fed," the wasted tissues restored. The mind must be kept quiet and there must be nothing to impede nature's course. The doctor's care would thus be devoted to the particular symptoms in this case, the best way to remedy them, and the immediate needs of the patient. His science would be brought to bear to understand the disease. Very little would be said at any time about the ultimate origin and permanent cure of nervous prostration.

The mental healer, on the other hand, would trace the trouble to worry, fear, wrong belief, disturbing mental pictures, and the like. He would not discuss symptoms. He would say nothing about "feeding the nerves," but would sit quietly by the patient day after day, holding before the mind a picture of this woman as perfect and in perfect health. He would give some advice in regard to the thoughts, but would at first say nothing about the theory of mental cure. The theory would be introduced more and more as the months passed and the sufferer gradually recovered. The doctor would trace the disease to disordered nerves. The mental healer would find its source in a disordered mind. Both, we will say, would be partly right, and nature would restore the patient in either case. The woman might be a trifle wiser in either event, but would she know how to live so that nervous prostration would be impossible?

Under either practice it is to be noted that the healer would be powerless to effect a sudden cure. The doctor would be too wise to expect it. The mental therapeutist might anticipate it, but it would not come. Temporary relief and a glossing over might come, but not a cure. There is a meaning, in this fact that recovery is gradual. It is a poor rule that does not apply in both directions. The disease came on even more gradually than it disappeared. But let us bear in mind that the present theory of disease is by no means hostile to the truth of spiritual healing. All the mental influences which we have considered in the foregoing chapters may be present and may be factors. The main point here emphasised is that all these influences, tendencies, and causes, as well as the physiological conditions, are relative to the soul which owns them. Investigation thus drives us deeper and deeper until, passing from the physiological to the mental conditions, we finally penetrate beneath the profoundest mental layer, or plane, and enter the realm of spiritual causation, or the attitudes of the soul.

Physical or natural causation may therefore be true in its own right. If I meet with an accident and break a leg or receive a cut, I need not ask, "What was I thinking?" Mental causation may also hold on its own plane, as when I misinterpret a painful sensation out of which I proceed to develop heart disease. But spiritual causation is also true. It is pure dogmatism to insist that causation is limited to any one realm. Therefore if we are to formulate a really profound theory we must start with the activities which are fundamental to all.

It is well known, for example, that many diseases are due to nervous shock. Whether or not a person suffers a violent nervous reaction in such a case depends upon the degree of composure. The degree of pain suffered depends upon the presence or absence of nervous tension. Fear is doubtless a factor in many cases, but fear gains the mastery only when there is lack of self-control. Pain may be enormously increased or greatly diminished by muscular rigidity, in the one case, and restful relaxation in the other. A sudden outburst of pain which would carry everything before it in some instances, by arousing the most terrible fears, would pass almost unnoticed in another instance when the meaning of the sensation was understood. Dyspepsia, catarrh, diseases of the lungs, rheumatism, paralysis, and a hundred other maladies are, relatively speaking, effects, externals, when compared with the mode of using the psycho-physiological forces whose disturbed equilibrium was the basis of these gradually developed conditions. For disease springs out of the whole life and must be studied from the point of view of the whole. There may be a dozen superficial diseases with specific names. Many physicians may try their skill in the removal of these conditions. But if there be one fundamental disease that is untouched these effects will re-appear when the treatment ceases.

To purify a stream we must penetrate to its first source. And back of all primal sources in every human being, without exception, there is a mode of meeting life which is fundamental to every phase of the individual's existence. Optimistic ideals may accompany natural restoration to health and seem to produce it, but there may be no necessary connection. All these factors may be influential but we are in search of the decisive factor. One point is clear all along. Every restorative process is primarily nature's instinctive effort to react, or regain equilibrium. The utmost any physician of any kind ever did was to aid in the removal of obstructions. It is a question of the kind of activity which best assists nature.

It is clear, then, that the direction of mind is not all. It is sometimes the controlling factor, but is at times itself controlled. People do not consciously think themselves into disease or simply "believe" they have a certain malady. The subconscious mind, wherein we revolve and make our own the ideas and impressions that come to us, is a far more potent factor in our experience than merely conscious thought. The influence of our opinions and habitual beliefs, our fears and traditional theories of disease, is so subtle, so closely connected with every aspect of life, that we are largely unconscious of its power over us. We do not see how our states of mind can affect bodily conditions; and consequently we do not include these subtle effects in our interpretations of disease, until we learn that the direction of mind often carries the energy of the organism with it. Human experience is in a sense what we make it by our thought, but to that one word "thought" must be added the whole life of man. Our inquiry has taught us little if it has not shown that experience is a union of objective and subjective elements; that even in the simple experience of physical sensation there is present not only the substantial basis for which the materialist contends, but also the thought which makes our life primarily mental. If the reader will bear this dual aspect of experience in mind, he cannot misunderstand this chapter.*

The point of view is obviously radically different from that of the mental therapeutist, since the emphasis is put upon activity rather than upon thought, and activity is both mental and physical.

It is clear that suffering is not a mere "state of mind," as the mental healers affirm, but is a condition of the entire individual. Everyone who has given much attention to the subject of disease from this broader point of view must be convinced of this. In fact, it makes little difference, in one sense, what the physical malady is called; for on the disposition of the patient depends the nature and intensity of the disease. Back of all chronic invalidism, for example, there is usually a disposition that is hard to influence, whose traits of character are made known in every aspect of the disease. On the other hand, an unselfish person, devoted to a life of self-denial, or one who is absorbed in congenial work, is apt to be freest from disease. Those who have time and money to be ill, those who live in and for themselves, and have nothing to take their consciousness away from physical sensation, never lack for some symptom out of which to develop ill-health.

The fact that so much depends on the temperament and beliefs of each individual renders it difficult fully to describe the causes of disease. Some people are so hard to influence in any way, so tenacious of a condition, that a simple malady may be worse than a much-dreaded disease in a case where the disposition is pliable. The organic structure is tight and unyielding in many cases. People are too exacting, too intense in thought and action, or too opinionated and self-assertive to be easily moved. In such cases the struggle is always severe when it comes, and nature has a hard task to overcome so much rigidity. Many suffer from mere want of the action that comes from physical exercise. Some live too much in the so-called "spiritual" phase of life, and are out of adjustment to the everyday life of the world. Others are starving for spiritual food, and are in need of mental quickening, if not of severe intellectual discipline. Narrow religious opinions have a cramping effect on the whole life, both mental and physical. The tendency to nervous hurry is responsible for a large proportion of the more modern ailments. People dwell in fixed and narrow directions of life, until they become "cranky" or insane.

Worry and fear play an important part in all varieties of disease, and some people have scarcely a moment's freedom from some tormenting belief or mental picture. Ill-will, want of charity, jealousy, anger, or any emotion which tends to draw one into self, to shut in and contract, is marked in its effect; for, if continued, it disturbs the whole organism, it is reflected in the subconscious life, and finally in the body, where it is treated as a purely physical disease. Unrealised ambition, suppressed grief, continued unforgiveness, habitual dwelling upon griefs and troubles instead of living above them, disappointments, and a thousand unsuspected causes, which impede the free and outgoing expression of the individuality, have a corresponding effect on the general life.

So much, then, for the mental and physical disturbances that bring about disease, so far as we are here concerned with them. Our chief concern is the mode of life that enables one to regain health and to keep it;. Here, again, the emphasis is put upon conduct, not upon mere thought.*

*I have developed these thoughts more in detail in "A Book of Secrets," chaps. vi.-xiii.

It is universally admitted that there is a natural healing power resident in the body. This power is common to all, or nearly all, forms of organised life; and by observation of the higher animals we have learned how thoroughly and quickly it cures under favourable conditions. Many people have learned to relax and to keep quiet, like the animals, giving nature a free opportunity to heal their maladies. No one has ever discovered limits to this power, and some are firmly convinced of its ability to heal nearly every disease. It can knit bones together. If one meets with an injury or merely gets a splinter into one's finger, this resident force immediately sets to work in accordance with certain laws. There is a gathering about the injured part, and an outward pressure tending to expel any obstacle foreign to the body. Everyone knows that the healing process is impeded or quickened according to the way we deal with it. The process is simple and fairly well understood, so far as a mere injury is concerned. We rely upon it, and know how to adjust ourselves to it. But what happens when the equilibrium of the body has been interfered with in another way, and the vital functions impeded? Do we wait as patiently for nature to heal us as when we meet with an accident? No, nine times out of ten we mistake its cause, call it a disease which we think we have "caught," misinterpret our sensations, and resist the very power which tries to heal us. This resistance, intensified by dwelling upon sensation and careful observation or symptoms, adds to the intensity of the suffering, until the trouble becomes pronounced, if not organic or chronic.

But, despite our resistance, the resident restorative power is ever trying to make itself known, ever ready to free the body from any obstacle or inharmony, and restore the natural equilibrium. It is continually purifying, cleansing, throwing off all that is foreign. It is trying to free us from any inheritance which may cause trouble or suffering. Wherever we are weak, unfinished, undeveloped, that weak point, that undeveloped state, or that animal residuum, is the seat of pressure from within of this same power, trying to make us better and purer. It ever penetrates nearer and nearer the centre of the organism. If one is exposed to the cold, to contagious disease, or whatever the influence, the power is still there to protect and to heal. In all natural functions the power is with us, fully competent to secure their free and painless activity. It works through instinct and impulse for our welfare. On a higher plane the evolutionary power is operative in character, urging us to be unselfish, to understand the law of growth, and to obey it. On the spiritual level it is ever ready to guide and to inspire us, but apparently not so aggressive here, since so much more depends on our receptivity and desire to learn. On all these planes the power is pressing upon us from within, trying to expand from a centre, as the rose-bud expands or as the seed develops when its resident life is quickened. Ultimately speaking, it is the power of God. It is beneficent, good, evolutionary, calling for trustful co-operation and restfulness on our part. We need not go anywhere or think ourselves anywhere to find it; for it is with us in every moment of experience, yet ordinarily unknown, rejected, and opposed.

If, then, it be asked why passion is so persistent, why evil has such power, why disease is so positive and real, there can be but one ultimate answer. The reality behind the appearance is to be found through acknowledgement of the values attributable to the life that is immanently active with us; the suffering, the evil, is largely due to our maladjustment to the immanent life, in our ignorance of its nature and its purpose with us. There is some obstacle, some inharmony to be overcome. The restorative power is trying to free us from it; and, when it comes in contact with it, friction results. There is an agitation made known to us as " pain." This sensation we resist, not understanding it; and it becomes painful in proportion to our resistance.

To illustrate. The case was reported not long ago of a woman who was suffering with severe neuralgia. In her despair she was walking the floor, and her physician said the pain would not be relieved for forty-eight hours. Word came to her from one who had learned that much suffering is due to resistance to the remedial power to "let it come." The effect was immediate. The lady had been nerving herself to endure the pain, thereby increasing the intensity which first caused it; and the message revealed the whole process to her. She relaxed mentally, and surrendered the hold by which she had tried to endure the pain, became quiet, and fell asleep. This case is typical of a thousand others.*

For this incident, as well as for many of the ideas in this chapter, I am indebted to Annetta G. Dresser, whose long experience with the sick led to this interpretation of suffering.

Again, those whose task it is to do considerable mental work learn after a time when they have worked long enough; for, if they worked beyond a certain point, they become aware of pressure in some part of the head, from which a reaction is likely to follow. This is especially noticeable in learning a new language, taking up a study requiring close concentration, or any new occupation, art, science, or any form of physical exercise to which one is unaccustomed. One is soon conscious of fatigue, because the task is a new one, and habits have not yet been formed. The general tendency is to give way to the feeling of fatigue. Many become discouraged at this point, and give up study or exercise, saying that it makes them tired, and they cannot bear it.

What is this sense of fatigue? It is evidently due to the calling of power into a new direction. The new life clarifies. It comes into contact with an uncultivated portion of the being, physical as well as mental; and, meeting with resistance, friction of some sort is the natural result. But this friction does not mean that one cannot exercise or study. It means the formation of a new habit and direction of mind, and the best work is done after one has passed this "hard place." It calls upon one to wait a while, and let the agitation cease, let the new power settle down and become one's own. It is nature telling one to be less intense for the moment, to extend the limit of one's activity little by little.

It is a mistake, then, to give way entirely to a feeling of fatigue and of pain. By yielding to it, one's attention is put upon it, with the result that it is increased, until the consciousness is absorbed in physical sensation. Rightly understood, pain is the conflict of two elements, a purer element coming in contact with a lower, and trying to restore equilibrium. Let us repeat. It is remedial. It is beneficent, the most beneficent of all nature's arrangements, the best evidence of the unceasing presence of a resident restorative power. Through it we are made aware that we have a Life not wholly our own that cares for us, and is capable, perfectly competent, to take us through any possible trouble, since it is there only for our own good, since it is itself thoroughly good.

It is obviously the power that one should think of, and not of the sensation. In this way, if one is determined to see the good, to think of the outcome, one will live out of and above the sensation; for all these thoughts help. The consciousness is either turned in one direction or in the other. It either helps or it hinders. One either moves with the current of life, or tries to stem it. In one direction the thought is turned into matter, in the other toward spirit. In one direction toward self, with a tendency to withdraw, shut in, contract; in the other, towards the higher Self who is telling us to be wiser.

The downward attitude may be illustrated by instances of suppressed grief, fear, or any emotion which causes one to draw into self. The natural restorative power tries to throw off that which has been suppressed. A gainful sensation in some part of the body is the result; and, mistaking the sensation, the mind, full of fear, contracts more intensely, thus causing the sensation to increase, until nature can only restore equilibrium by a violent reaction, which receives the name of some well-known disease.

But why do we resist?, why do we draw into the consciousness of physical sensation? Obviously, because we are ignorant of the immanent Life that is moving upon us. We have been educated to believe that disease is a physical entity. The fears and sympathetic words of friends help the process. The possible symptoms we are likely to suffer are graphically described, the memory of past experiences of suffering is recalled, until finally the whole diseased condition is pictured before us, and the thought is every moment becoming more firmly fixed in the wrong direction. The mind once established in the wrong direction, the activities of the entire organism respond.

It is important to note that one cannot judge by physical sensation, but should look beyond it. In sensitive natures the pain is very much exaggerated, and is no guide at all. Sometimes the sensation is so keen and the pressure is reduced to such a fine point that one's consciousness is like a caged bird fluttering about in a vain endeavour to escape. Shut in there with such intense activity, the wildest fears are aroused when there is no reason for alarm. The trouble is simply very much restricted. The resident Life is pressing through a very narrow channel; and relief will come in due time if one is quiet, patient, not trying to endure the pain, but letting nature complete its task.

When the emotions are touched, the struggle is intense, and is more likely to be misunderstood. The immanent Life, moving upon man where he is weak and undeveloped, through instinct, passion, and impulse, produces restlessness, which in turn causes him to rush now into this thing and now into that, and perhaps commit a deed which from another point of view is called a "crime," even before he is aware of what he is doing. The very tendencies and instincts which would guide him in his development, if he understood them, are misdirected. An impulse blesses or curses, according to the attitude towards it, the way in which it is followed, blindly or intelligently. Man never conquers himself by self-suppression anymore than by indulgence, but by adjustment.

The meaning of much of our moral suffering and evil is, then, to teach the right use of our powers; and moral misery and degradation will probably continue until the lesson is learned. All cases of sickness, misery, evil, call for better self-comprehension. If there be one meaning which may be found in them all, it is, in one word, progress,—the effort of the Spirit to give us freedom. If we understood this, we should have a larger sympathy and charity for the whole human race, and be spared much suffering over the sins and crimes of others, and should look for the meaning, the Spirit, behind all wrong acts and all degraded lives.*

There are, of course, many other problems involved. The present discussion is devoted to an underlying interest.

The great question, then, in all problems of suffering and evil, regarded from the point of view of values and ideals, is this: What is God doing with us? What is the ideal toward which the immanent Life is moving? All secondary questions reduce themselves to this; for everything goes to show that the universe is a system, an organism, an adjustment of means to ends for the benefit and development of the whole, inspired by one grand purpose. We did not make the world order. We cannot change it; and, if our life in it is full of misery, it is for us to discover how we make that misery, how we rebel, how we resist, and what the order means, in and through our lives. If a nation is torn by internal troubles, by wars and wrangling of conflicting parties, it is evident that it has not yet learned the great lesson of human brotherhood, and that its troubles must continue in one form or another until it discovers what the evolutionary energy means, what it is trying to make known through these conflicts. Contest and controversy will continue in the same way between science and religion, between the great religions and the sects into which many religions are divided, until men learn that all truth is one and universal, and does not depend on any book or any person, but is the inherent property of all, trying to make itself known through these very controversies, revealed in every fact of life. Theory and practice will also be at variance until it is clear that in a sense they are profoundly one, that what a man does he believes, regardless of his boasted theory. Impulse or instinct will be man's guide until he learns what is behind it, until he stops to reflect and act intelligently with, not against, the higher forces of his being; for thoughtlessness is the besetting sin of man. A large proportion of the crimes committed by him would be prevented if he stopped to consider the consequences, not only the suffering which would be caused to others, but his own severe punishment, caused solely by his own acts.

From the point of view of values and ideals, we may therefore say that, suffering is intended to make man think. Behind all experience moves one great aspiring Power, developing and perfecting the world. It moves straight towards its goal unceasingly and without permanent hindrance. Wherein man is adjusted to it, he is already free from suffering. He moves with it, and knows how to be helped by it. But wherein he still acts ignorantly, he suffers, and is sure to be in conflict until he understands the law of growth.

Man has been defined as "a pleasure-loving animal." He is lazy, and will postpone thinking for himself or try to shift his responsibility until he learns that everything depends on the development of individuality. But a day comes when he begins to reflect and to see the meaning of it all. Everywhere, in the outer world, in history, in politics, in religion, he finds two forces contending with each other. Turning to his own nature, he finds the same, a higher, rational, moral and spiritual self contending with a lower, an impulsive, animal self. He sees that he must obey the one and neglect the other, or, better, lift the other to a higher plane. He sees that evil is a relative term,* depending on our point of view, and that conduct which seems perfectly justifiable on one plane of existence is condemned on a higher plane, where different standards prevail. It becomes clear that virtue or goodness can only be attained through an experience full of contrasts and friction, an experience which calls out the best that is in us,—true sympathy, love, and character. The meaning of his own mysterious past becomes clear. He sees the rich compensation for all that he has suffered in the wisdom and character it has brought him. And, finally, in this far-reaching adjustment of means to ends he recognises the love of God, and proves to his own satisfaction that love really dwells at the heart of the universe.

*This is, of course, no excuse for it.

The discovery, then, that there is no escape from the operation of cause and effect, neither mental nor physical, is a turning-point in the progressive career of man; for the majority still persuade themselves that they will somehow be excused. Suffering is necessary only to bring us to a knowledge of the law, to bring us to a certain point; and it will persist until that point is reached. Our experience of today is largely conditioned by our past life. It is what we have passed through which makes it possible for us to stand where we do today. Consequently, what we do and think today will largely govern our experience of tomorrow and of all future days. Fate has not decided everything for us, after all; for it was by our own consent, unconsciously, thoughtlessly, and consciously, that we suffered. Our fate is, that through our individuality something is bound to come forth, since the resistless power of Almighty God is behind it. Our freedom lies in choosing whether to move with this progressive tendency or against it; for man may evidently continue to oppose and misuse the power that would bless him. He may postpone the lesson which at some time and somewhere he must learn. If, then, in any case the result will sometime be the same, it is matter of economy to learn the real course of events as soon as possible.

As hard, then, as it may seem to be compelled to suffer the results of unwise conduct, it is through this discovery that we learn the meaning of suffering and the way out of it. Once more, then, we must look beyond physical sensation to the conscious man behind it, choosing, willing, acting, determining his conduct, and his pain or pleasure, by his direction of mind. It is impossible in one chapter to consider suffering in all its phases; but, if this central thought is clear, if the reader has stopped to consider the intimate relationship of God to man in every moment of life, these neglected problems will be equally clear.

Not all suffering is evolutionary. Not every evil act has its discernible meaning. Most of our suffering is purely incidental, and passes off without leaving us any the wiser; but all suffering, all evil, may become evolutionary. Every experience will teach us something if we question it, and will yield its message of hope.

Finally, then, it is clear that for each of us the question of suffering is a matter of experience, and that all theories of it must be empirically tested. For here, far more than in any other domain of life, theory avails little; it is what we actually prove that settles the question. "They that are well need no physician." Those who have not had the first inkling of mental influences are often most quickly benefited by the superficial doctrines of mental therapeutists. But those who have lived and suffered deeply know that it is life, not theory, that avails. It is when some deepening experience comes, an experience that proves the utter superficiality of all merely mental theories, that we begin to make the great transition from appearance to reality. Suffering is a reality. It has to do with the deepest powers and interests of our nature. Mere thinking about it will not suffice. It is impossible to advance one step farther than we have individually wrestled, tested, tried, proved, and conquered. One of course needs all the assistance which optimism can give. It is sometimes necessary to make affirmations even in the face of facts. But the essential is not the thought, but the deed; not the suggestion, but the attitude.

Philosophy and practice are at one here. There is no reason for saying that the universe is merely an affair of thought. Man is far more than a thinker. God is infinitely more than the idea of God. Life is real, life is earnest, it is substantial. God is power. Man is an active being. The universe is a theatre of forces. Thoughts come and go, but deeds abide. Thought is reflective, imitative, secondary; it interprets, seeks to understand. It is power, life, that is primary—when force meets force, and life meets life. Only by thinking can one understand. But only by doing may one accomplish. Hence thought must not forget what it sought to understand. Man must not forget to refer back to experience and test theory by practice. It is on the level of power that one comes into relation with the immanent Life. It is that Life, together with our reactions upon it, that has made us what we are. Therefore, since "conduct is three-fourths of life," it is by wiser conduct that one at last solves the problem of suffering.

Chapter IX
Duality of Self

—

ONE of the most strongly marked characteristics of the inner life is the play of moods, the duality of self. The pages of religious literature abound in accounts of ineffable visions wherein the seers have beheld God face to face, as it were. But almost invariably there follow descriptions of mental states which are anything but sublime. The highest and lowest moods are sometimes found in one individual. The more emotional the temperament the greater seems to be the contrast. The majority of such people are creatures of moods. It seldom occurs to them that it is possible to understand the psychology of moods, and that by the aid of this psychology one may master these emotional fluctuations and co-ordinate the self. Co-ordination is intellectual and requires systematic thinking, and those who are the victims of contrasted emotions seldom possess the intellectual development that is required for such mastery, Nor does it usually occur even to those in whom the struggle is less intense to make a study of the conditions under which the higher visions come in order to know how to cultivate them.

The majority of us live in fragments. The mind is a chaos. The sublime and the ridiculous mingle. There is neither system nor beauty. We are not only prisoners of ideas but creatures of whims, fears, and sentiments. Today, under the influence of certain circumstances, we express a decided opinion. Tomorrow, another mood succeeds and we wonder that we could have voiced yesterday's sentiments. Now we are hopeful, now despondent. Yesterday we could accomplish nothing. Today everything is plastic before us. Now we doubt and now we believe. We are first credulous, then extremely cautious. One friend sways us, others have no power except to follow where we lead. Thus contrast pursues contrast from day to day, and inconsistency is ever a marked characteristic of our thoughts, words, and deeds.

But these are only the minor contrasts. There are greater inconsistencies which our lips seldom confess, though our actions constantly betray us. Each of us is at once an angel and a devil—in embryo at least. Upon occasion we may be extremely courteous, gracious, charitable, and forgiving. We deny ourselves—if the sacrifice be not too great. We voice noble sentiments and sometimes approach genuine inspiration. But let a novel occasion arise, let someone attack a person who is dear as life itself, let it be a time of danger or a great threatening calamity, and we can be as fierce as a savage animal. And who that aspires after holy things has not faced a tendency within him which is as incongruous with and hostile to these holy desires as hate is hostile to love?

It is needless to dwell upon this contrast. Every man knows what it is to possess the two natures. Every honest person admits their conflict. Many a refined individual is weighed down with grief because the animal or devil is present, when only the angel is desired. Nearly everyone is mystified by these persistent obsessions of the lower nature. And countless souls have cried out in despair, as the conflict has continued from year to year, "How long, O Lord, how long?"

The majority of men and women give more or less complete expression to one mood or the other when it arises, and their doctrines are such attempts at harmony between the moods as their incongruous character permits. If the lower nature, or at least some fleshly or pathological condition, is largely dominant in a philosophic mind, the pessimistic mood is likely to colour the philosophy. If the higher nature is more frequently triumphant we may have an optimist. Thus our human doctrines are frequently mere reports of the discolourations of our moods.

This is of course a familiar thought and need not be considered at length. Nor need we emphasise the fact that in many cases the disconsolate mood merely points to a disordered stomach, liver, or brain. The essential idea for us is the possibility that a man may become so conscious of the deflections wrought by disease, by the power of other minds, by environment, and the like, that he can conquer these deflecting states and pass beyond them.

We have already acquired this art to some extent. We know from experience that emotion is apt to be ephemeral and temporarily disruptive, therefore we let the sun set on our wrath. We are aware of the subtleties of personal infatuation, and so we seek entire solitude when we wish to know what we truly think and whom we really love. When ill we know that life wears an entirely different aspect, that it is not a time to propound a philosophy of the universe. Life seems almost incredibly different in the slums and in a society drawing-room. It matters much whether all our bills are paid, and we have a bank account or whether we know not where the next dollar is coming from. With all these deflecting tendencies we are more or less familiar, and we have learned to guard against them. But need we stop here? Is a man who in one mood believes all things spiritual and good, and who in the next knows not why he believes, yet a complete man? What if he should study to put himself into the creative mood, that he may conquer the unphilosophical? A daring suggestion you say, this proposal to master one's genius, but let us pursue the hypothesis awhile.

Let us divide all moods into two general types, which we will for convenience classify as lower and higher. Let us say, figuratively speaking, that the soul dwells on two general levels on each of which there is a thought stream. The illustration closely conforms to the facts of our inconsistent moods.

The lower level of consciousness is life in sensation, in matter, mere facts; the higher is the plane of insight, the realm of ideals, values. On the lower level the soul is under the law and is painfully conscious of it; on the higher it is in the attitude of the victor. The lower states are characterised by a sense of limitation; there is a painful awareness of the process that is going on. In the higher state one sees the goal toward which the process is tending. All that was so painfully apparent on the lower level is now seen, and far more. The attention is put upon the ideal of the soul as the master. Suffering is regarded in the light of its significance in the growth of character, Material possessions are valued only for what they are worth.

From the lower point of view, life is seen as a conflict, where there is constant hating and fighting. From above, strife is seen in the light of the peace which is its outcome. The lower is the plane of temptation, the higher is the domain of that quiet composure which overcometh. The one is a closing-in, selfish attitude; the other is out-going, unselfish. The lower is the realm of judgment from the appearance, of physiological diagnosis; the higher is characterised by righteous judgment. The judgments that are based on the lower states may be perfectly true on their own level. But from the higher point of view they may be utterly reversed.

For example, take the readings of a person's character that are based on phrenology, palmistry, graphology, and astrology. No doubt the character is written in the hand, marked upon the face, and indicated by the shape of the head; and physical man is of course related to the stars. Granted that the exponent of these systems of character-reading is able to read every sign correctly, many valuable facts may thus be learned. But suppose an astrologist were able to read the future with strictest accuracy—and there is always room for the gravest doubt—would it follow that the prophecy would come true? The prophecy might be mathematically exact on its own plane. It might be that if the man in question should keep down on the level of astrological influences, he would meet precisely the circumstances foretold. But if he chanced to be one who knows how to lift his activities to the spiritual level, the influences in question might pass as impotently by as a temptation to take intoxicating liquor passes by a virtuous man who is not for a moment prompted to respond. For astrological influences undoubtedly touch only the surfaces of a man's life. A man might indeed come in contact with such influences and conquer them. But he might as easily be entirely unaware of them. Thousands of influences pass impotently by because there is no point of contact in the individual.

A friend once wrote me a pitying letter because, as he said, there were many "malefics" round about, and I must be having "a trying time," financially and otherwise. I answered that I was not aware of the presence of any "malefics," that I was moving along contentedly, quite happy in my studies. My friend at once replied that inadvertently he had neglected to take Jupiter's influence into account; that Jupiter's power overcame that of the "malefics." But what if another planet were able to overcome Jupiter? To what lengths must one qualify in order to obtain astrological truth?

Now, whatever the truth in diagnoses, readings, and prophecies based on the study of external influences, the ultimate question is this: What is the highest influence? If the influences of the lower level are relative to that level, obviously one can place no ultimate reliance on them. To the extent that one is aware of superior influences one may entirely neglect the lower order of forces. In general, the lower is the realm of fate, the higher the realm of freedom. Astrologers, palmists, and all similar "prophets" strenuously resist the reproach of fatalism. Yet it is practically impossible for them to avoid its subtle power.

Our little excursion into the region of the "pseudo-sciences" may serve as an illustration of the endless relativities that beset the lower level of consciousness. The great lesson is this: one cannot judge by sensation, given condition, present influence. A thousand things seem true, while one is immersed in sense, that prove utterly false when the vision is once more cleared. Such judgments are like the opinions of the social settlement worker whose mind is utterly weighed down by thought of the dreadful situation of dwellers in the slums. It is one thing to know the facts; it is quite another to see their true bearing. It is doubtless well to become acquainted with man's actual situation in life, but there is no help for us while we dwell solely upon the darker side.

The moral of course is easily drawn: one should push through into the sunlight, live on the higher level as much as possible, hold to the ideal, dwell on the outcome, not on the details of the evolutionary process. Yet there is a lesson to be learned from both points of view. It is through the alternation of moods that one at last sees the law. Today, for example, I am conscious on the lower level. Bodily conditions weigh upon me and a flood of thoughts expressive of my depressed condition rush into mind. Tomorrow, the weight lifts and I rise to the superior plane. All the world is transformed. I laugh at the follies and fears of yesterday. My vision carries me many times as far. I behold all that I saw yesterday and a vast extent of territory beyond. I must qualify or enlarge all my conclusions of yesterday. I now deem myself sane and rational. Never more can doubts assail me. But no, in my zeal I have overleaped the mark. Tomorrow I am down again. Yet it is an enlarged tomorrow and I correct the enthusiasm of today. The day following I rise again, bearing the memory of these instructive contrasts. By continuing to compare I gradually develop a well-poised mood which is larger than either the customary lower or the temporary higher state.

The more comprehensive mood is thus a product of experience tempered and developed by reflection. It is my servant, my instrument; whereas the other moods mastered me. It profits by the experiences of both and thus gradually achieves what men ordinarily deem impossible. For note that those in whom the duality is most strongly marked are extremists. They are either decidedly happy or most miserable. In a thousand ways they veer from extreme to extreme. Observers of such people set them down as extremists and the people themselves suppose that they must accept the inevitable.

My proposition is that the greater the tendency towards extremes the more poised may the individual become. It is by lacking moderation and repose that the self-conscious extremist learns the need and value of poise. Thus the place and meaning of suffering are seen. Thus pain is only understood when we pass beyond it. For remember that it is not so much what we are born with but what we attain, what we overcome, which teaches life's lesson and gives us wisdom to contribute to the world.

This truth is seldom recognised, however. If one eulogises poise, moderation, and equanimity, people exclaim, "Oh, you were born with it. Preach not to us of your gift." They cannot believe that one who is now serene was once storm-tossed. Yet we have relatively little appreciation for the virtues with which we were born. Those who thus ridicule the advocate of self-control and equanimity little suspect that this same serene preacher was once extremely excitable and has persistently laboured for a score of years to acquire the repose he now possesses. They do not remember that the mind learns by contrast and grows by mastering opposites.

It is no small task to master a mood which once swayed you. But this is the progressive possibility which awaits those who learn the meaning of their lower and higher mental states. At first one notes only the contrast. Then the great discovery is made that excess on one plane means excess on the other. As surely as a reaction follows intemperate passion and all that makes us devils, so does ecstasy of spiritual emotion cause a descent to the animal plane. Everyone can testify to this who has yielded himself to undue emotional zeal.

Scepticism, agnosticism, self-condemnation morbid consciousness of sin, and a thousand other similar states, are simply excessive reactions from their opposites. If we do not believe too much we do not doubt. When we have not been immoderately negative in our thinking we do not become agnostics. Self-condemnation becomes morbid when we have dwelt too long on one idea. We believe ourselves "hopeless sinners" only while we are negligent of our nobler possibilities.

The mystery of our dual nature is half solved when we learn that these violent contrasts are due to excess on the one side or the other. The next step is to begin by daily practice to acquire a centre of equilibrium, apart from the domination of either lower or higher mood, where one may take one's stand and call a halt every time the limit of moderation is reached.

There is no vicarious salvation in this kind of world. It is downright work and plenty of it that wins the prize. All the wisdom that other systems offer is useful. But now at last one must conquer self. Nine times out of ten, at first, we forget when immersed in the clouds that there is daylight above. When the bright sun shines we forget that night must come. Thus wofully short-sighted, we blunder along. It is no wonder that we cannot give a reason for the faith that is in us.

But suppose we begin a series of observations, precisely as the chemist observes the behaviour of certain liquids to discover their laws. Let us note the conditions when, or immediately after, the higher mood is on. Then let us remember that those conditions will come again, even though a lower mood ensues. If you observe serenely when the flood time of spiritual life comes you will find that you do not sink so low. If you face it calmly, when your lower self presents a temptation, you will husband energy and acquire power to overcome it. Every time you consciously rise from the lower to the higher plane you make headway in the development of a new habit—the art of self-control, of spiritual self-mastery.

Thus little by little you will transmute your energy, until victories which once seemed discouragingly impossible will become easy. After a time when a pessimistic, fleshly, or selfish tendency arises you will instantly know it, and will turn the tide then and there. You will marvel that you once permitted yourself to be a slave of moods and tendencies over which you now possess great power. You will look back upon your moody years as years of infancy.

What is the secret of the turning from lower to higher? The foregoing discussions show that it is voluntary attention, not the attention that is compelled by a mental or physical state, but the attention which breaks loose from the state that would hold it and actively concentrates itself upon a mental picture, ideal, or recollected experience which centralises the consciousness upon the higher plane.

How or when is it possible thus voluntarily to shift attention? When there is sufficient repose in the self to become poised, to take hold of one's self and turn the tide. Thus cultivation of inner poise, peace, is the prime essential. Remember that repose begins to come with knowledge of these contrasted mental states, and that actual headway is made when one actively begins to pause, to hold still, to gather momentum and husband energy. Then an undesirable mental state arises one is able to shift attention from the state to the remembered higher experience. To shift the attention is to transfer the balance of power to the higher plane where all the forces of that life-stream come forward to aid. To shift the attention is to give a new direction to action or conduct.

But how shall one invite the higher states denoted "spiritual," the sources of inspiration, for the development of poise? By the formulation and constant renewing of ideals which, if confidently held, give new tendencies to the subconscious mind. Where man's desires are concentrated there his activities congregate. If a man longs for that which is spiritual his very desire will tend to bring it. The subconscious mind will be shaped by this the strongest conscious desire. Thus the balance of power is once more transferred from lower to higher.

At first life is disintegrated. We are loosely put together. Our thought is chaotic. Therefore the world seems chaotic. But note how systematic, orderly, that man finds the world who is well-knit, precise, methodical. He has a place for everything and all of his facts are classified; when he delivers philosophic discourses his thought is subdivided into books, chapters, sections, heads, and subheads. He may not inspire you as does the more erratic man of genius. But his thought is immensely instructive, owing to the fact that he finds the world what he is, what his life is—a system.

Our ideal synthesis would be no less systematic, but it would leave an entire section for data even now getting themselves reported, and another section for possible coming events which have not yet cast the dimmest shadow before. Thus there are possibilities of ever broader and broader co-ordinations. The essential is this: become co-ordinated. Remedy the defect in yourself that you may more truly contemplate the world. If the world seems sound and sweet, become sweet and sound that you may know the world. If your bias is towards one pole, study the lives and the philosophy of those who gravitate to the other. The perfect whole we must have. At any rate we must try that hypothesis, we must become as nearly sane as our organic limitations permit. If we learn that they really are limitations we shall see beyond them.

The theory of life which we are here advocating is an organic view as compared with the output of a single mood such as optimism or pessimism. We are declaring that such a view is impossible without co-ordination of life. This is tantamount to saying that a man shall know truth only so far as he practises virtue, the many-sided virtue of beauty, symmetry. If a philosopher would solve his speculative problems, let him then take a step in advance in his life. If he would know how to take this step let him test this proposition: A spiritual or philosophical state of mind has an unconscious or subconscious dynamic value. To regain this higher state one may either put one's self in a spiritually receptive mood, or gradually think one's self there by philosophising. With the exalted thought comes an exalted feeling. Gently, moderately, enter into and possess this sentiment and rest there. Do not merely think about eternity, about peace, and beauty, and love. But feel yourself one with love at peace, in eternity—a beautiful soul. Do not underestimate yourself. Do not condemn or despise yourself. Think not now of the weight of years and the burdens of inheritance. These higher thoughts of yours are actual intimations of immortality. "My words are spirit and are life." Peace and joy be with you—the peace of God, and the joy that knows no reaction.

This is all very well as a statement of religious mood, the student may reply, but this does not show that there is a mood large enough to embrace all the contrasts, contradictions, and incongruities of our dual nature. No, I reply, but it is a long step in advance. I am outlining a method of advance: the argument is not yet complete. We have seen that the conflicts of the lower and higher moods are the chief sources of doubt that any mood is universal. Now, in so far as we understand these contrasts within ourselves and learn to conquer them, we make a great gain. By becoming more moderate, better balanced in our lives, we acquire that insight by which the apparently incongruous is unified. We understand more and more clearly the reason for the faith that is in us. Our moods believe in each other more and more. For we rise above their limitations and see far beyond them to their common background. Thus we are less and less subject to moods and better able to create desirable mental states, by giving our thoughts and feelings a timely turn. The philosophical co-ordination which thus results is superior in value even to the mood of unconscious inspiration where one dwells on supernal heights. Even this highest spiritual state comes more under the will, for although one cannot always invite it directly, one can at least prepare the mind subconsciously for its coming.

We have found that the starting-point is acuter knowledge of self; and that the next step is the development of poise, inner peace, tranquillity. Obviously one's daily life must be adapted with this end in view. Then we have found that the poised inner centre becomes the basis of self-control, that self-mastery means the triumph over moods, the adjustment of lower and higher tendencies, and finally that this prepares the way for greater triumphs over the flesh.

The meaning of life for each of us is thus clearly seen. Each of us is an individual with an experience in some sense unique. We exist, at least in this life, for the discovery, development, and value of that experience. The mere facts of life at any one time, however trying, however severely we may suffer, are not true signs of what we are or why we are here. We should not judge by our pathological condition. We should not measure the world by our despair or pain. The true self is the possessor of all these moods, the true significance of our experience is their total meaning, and these moods are one and all means to ends in the process of self-development.

Your life then has a meaning. There is a reason why you are here. You are needed. Know yourself, then, that you may learn what you stand for in relation to other men. Develop your individuality, then contribute its organic wisdom to the philosophy of humanity. Remember that the respects in which you are negative, weak, undeveloped, are as likely, if not more likely, to afford opportunity for growth, and hence for addition to your wisdom. Your passion shall instruct you. Even the devil in you shall lift you on his shoulders to a higher level. Do not therefore condemn yourself. Regard everything as an advantage, that is, derive advantage from everything.

What then has been regarded as a basis of doubt is here taken to be reason for faith. That is, the limitations of temperament have been deemed such that each of us could never obtain more than a temperamental view of truth. Thus philosophers have discarded the most valuable means and have arrived at negative results. But the art of philosophy should precede the fuller science. We should first conquer and help others to conquer, then rationalise our victories. We must so master the moods in us which discolour the world for us that we shall be able as it were to stand in front of our coloured glasses. In this way only are we ever likely to see the full meaning of our aches and pains, our wilfulness and deviltry.* For we must truly be in order truly to know. If we would really know God we must practise the presence of God. If we would know the reasons for the faith that is in us, we must persistently study ourselves in the act of faith. Thus shall we gradually grow in power, and power shall lead to wisdom.

*The psychological study of religion is important in connection with the problems of this chapter. Among the best books are: "The Psychology of Religion," E. D. Starbuck, Scribners, 1900; "The Spiritual Life," Prof. Coe, Eaton & Mains, 1900; "The Soul of a Christian," Prof. F. Granger, Macmillan, 1900; and Prof. William James's "Varieties of Religious Experience," Longmans, Green & Co., 1902.

Chapter X
Adjustment

—

IN one of the most secluded of Alpine valleys, where the steam whistle has never broken the native stillness, nor the progress of science intruded on the confines of medieval tradition, lies one of the most remarkable villages in the world. As the traveller enters this unique town, he feels that he has suddenly stepped into another world; for the people inspire him with an unwonted reverence, and an atmosphere of Sabbath stillness rests over all the valley. One all-controlling idea pervades the town, and is alike absorbing to every man, woman, and child who lives there. The village is Oberammergau; and here once in ten years representatives of all civilisation come to witness the renowned Passion Play. For hundreds of years this play has been given ten summers in a century by these simple peasants, and their entire lives are devoted to preparation for it. To take the part of the Christ is the summit of their ambition. They feel it a solemn duty to give the play, and from childhood their lives are shaped by this ambition. In order to portray a certain character, they practise the most careful self-denial. They try to mould their lives in accordance with the qualities of that character, they dwell on it and rehearse it year in and year out. And this is why they are so remarkable. They are shaped by an ideal. They have one object in view, and in their peasant simplicity and catholic faith they are willing to exclude every other. When they take part in the play, they make no affectation. They simply represent in actual life what they have so long dwelt upon as an ideal. And this ideal has left its stamp on everything associated with the town and its people.

It is a rare privilege for the student of the human mind to be among these people for a time, and to witness the play; for there in actual practice and in striking simplicity is the ideal of all character-building, of all co-operation with evolution, of all adjustment to life, namely, to have an object in view which one never loses sight of, which one gradually realises, day by day and year by year. Life for the most of us is vastly more complicated than for the peasant of Oberammergau; but the principle of character-building is the same, and might be made as simple and effective.

What this principle is we have been considering from the outset of our inquiry. We awaken into experience to find ourselves members of a great world-order. We live a twofold life, in part describable in mental terms, in part physical. When we awaken to consciousness of the vast process and begin to philosophise, we learn that we have made individual headway in so far as we have actively lived and thought. More or less ignorant of the forces that play upon us, we have been the victims of our own folly. Now that we are awake at last, we may begin intelligently to live. The same law that explains our past suffering makes clear the way to freedom. Whatever we have thought and done, we have been ever carried forward by the great organism of life. Now that we have learned this great fact, we may begin to move forward wisely and harmoniously. Whatever the nature of the experience, it matters greatly how we take it. Hence the future is largely in our hands.

In the light of the foregoing discussion, it is clear that at every step we must distinguish between the present conditions of our life and the ideal end towards which these conditions are apparently tending; between the lower self and the higher. In proportion as we make this discrimination and obey the higher self, are we free from conflict and suffering, adjusted to life. If we abandon our fears, cease to complain and rebel; if we learn the economy of our situation in life, then this higher self meets no opposition. Its purpose is made known without suffering. Then we begin to enjoy true freedom in co-operation with the omnipresent Helper, whom we once despised. Gradually, a simple system of conduct and of adjustment takes shape in our minds, until, like the peasant preparing to take part in the play, we know no other ideal. To suggest this ideal so far as one person may indicate it to another is the purpose of this chapter. In the first place, let us make sure that we understand how conduct is shaped by an idea. When we leave home, for instance, to go to the business portion of the town or city in which we live, it is usually because we have some definite object in view. Our conduct for the time is guided by a transient desire; and, in order to carry out this desire, we adjust ourselves to a certain arrangement of natural phenomena, and make use of certain mechanisms invented by man. We take a car or carriage. We are compelled to follow certain streets in order to reach our destination. We must avoid collision with other people, with electric cars and carriages. We must good-naturedly take the situation as we find it. And all these actions are governed, almost unconsciously, by a single desire; and we keep this end in view until we realise the desire.

Thus we might analyse the conduct of any day or any moment, and find that wish or desire is largely fundamental. When learning a language, we keep the object in view of reading and speaking it with fluency, and work for years until we attain the desired end. We make an invention because we need or desire it. The need or desire opens to us the means of fulfilling our wish. The artist has an ideal in view which he is ever striving to realise on canvas or in marble. Literature takes such form as our desires give it, modified by the degree of cultivation we have attained. We change the character of our buildings, of our homes, of our institutions, our philosophy, our religion, our conceptions of the divine nature, as rapidly as we ourselves change, and to the degree that our ideals and circumstances are modified by these inner changes. We endeavour to understand nature, life, history, our entire surroundings better. We then readjust ourselves in conformity with our better wisdom. And in every wise readjustment we are compelled to adopt nature's sure and measured method of evolution.

Thus far we have considered the self largely in its voluntary forms. We turn now to the spontaneous and more intimately divine phases of consciousness and of our ideals. For in deepest truth our desires and ideals are only partly our own. What we will to be in our hearts is closely related to what God would have us be. Our psychology must include the divine. This is the point of departure from the theorists who describe the universe in terms of mere thought, of personal affirmation and denial; and now we are in a position to emphasise the facts on which this departure is based.

As revealed in one's individual life—which in turn becomes a clue to world-life—the decisive point is the fact of guidance. Now, whether one deems it the voice of excarnate spirits or angel guides, the presence of Jesus, the direct word of God, or merely intuition in an impersonal sense, the fact is that guidances come, and that by paying attention to them they grow in power and frequency.

These guidances relate to affairs of daily life, the leading into an occupation, friendships and other associations. For example, one is conscious of a desire to do a certain work; the way unexpectedly opens and one is led to the right associates in what seems like a providential way. Again and again the way opens in due course where all seemed dark. One comes out at the top where it seemed inevitable that one must sink exhausted at the bottom. In numberless ways one's fears prove groundless, all plans prove needless and all doubts absurd. The guidances come year by year and the memory of them is subconsciously cherished until there flows up from below a flood of evidence amounting to an irresistible conviction, namely, that all things are working together toward one high and noble end. In contrast with this deeper current of life, the whims, thoughts, desires, and plans of the personal self are now seen to be superficial. It is no wonder that the passing finite moods are incongruous and fragmentary. The true unity is beyond the personal self; these passing whims and moods are inevitably disjointed.

Thus there is vouchsafed in due course a vision of the harmony of things where all that is of greatest value in life is beheld as one piece—not as a mosaic, but as a great rhythmic activity. I do not say that all our consciousness is beheld as one. He has slight acquaintance with the dualities of his inner life who has not discovered that he does not always obey the guidance, and that he sometimes mistakes the human and the divine. Simultaneously, there exist both the inner rhythm which the soul may express in poetic adjustment, in harmonious hexameters; and the human activity which may lead to discordant side-issues. The honest soul is so conscious of a lower tendency warring in the members so that when he would do good he does not or cannot, that he cries out, "How long must this conflict endure?" He knows that there are two wills, therefore he says, "Father, not my will, but Thine be done!"

To receive guidance is not then necessarily to obey it. Usually we find out what are guidances by retrospectively discovering the folly of not obeying them. Human experience would have no real value if we could do naught but obey. There is a long range of differences between the animal man who is contented in his animality, the sinner who is ignorant and wilful enough to glory in his sin; and the enlightened man who is making the transition from human waywardness to adjustment with the divine and who is literally doing the best he knows. The majority of us are too painfully conscious of our shortcomings to permit the fond delusion to creep in that everything we do is divinely inspired. We know well enough that there is a higher way and we are most eager to move in it. The more common error of really enlightened people is to make too hard work of it. The present discussion is specially designed to indicate the easier way, namely, by adjustment with evolution and reliance on the subconscious mind.

With the majority, the higher guidances are doubtless spontaneous at first. But by observing certain conditions one learns to prepare consciously for them. Mrs. Howe doubtless wrote The Battle Hymn because of a more or less conscious desire, which worked in her subconscious mind until, in the quietness of the night, the completed hymn welled into consciousness. Having observed the conditions spontaneously, one may consciously impress desires on the mind with the prayer that may be first subconsciously, then consciously realised. One may confidently seek the same guidance on any subject, and as confidently expect light, or help, or a "hymn."

For example, instead of painfully reasoning, seeking advice, and consulting theoretical treatises, one who desires the higher guidance should confidently ask, as of the great universe, how things are, what is right, whither to turn. The soul is thus opened more directly to know the divine tendency of things. It seeks knowledge by sight rather than by reasoning. It asks, What is? One can in this way even obtain guidance in advance of experience.

Now I do not mean that all that the soul is to do is already decided. But that there is a guidance which will lead us as directly as the bee-line instinct of an animal, if we become open to and implicitly follow it. Suppose I am contemplating a trip to Europe. I am eager to do what is right, therefore I try to rise above all merely personal desires and tendencies. I try to put myself into the rhythmic current of things, I seek the eternal order, I endeavour to commit my plans to the subconscious realm. To attain this receptivity I therefore isolate myself as fully as possible from my external environment. It is as though I could rise above the clouds on a stormy day to a height from which it is possible to see hundreds of miles. From that point I can actually foresee certain changes in the weather before they come. All the conditions are there to produce those conditions. I see much that is hidden from men on earth. Likewise in the invisible world I look far ahead and behold myself crossing the ocean and travelling about in safety. The conviction comes to me that it is wise to go. The conviction harmonises with conscience, with my sense of the fitness of things. Therefore I feel confidently inclined to start.

Moreover one's conviction is strengthened by the remembrance of similar experiences all of which tend to prove that "all things work together for good for them that love the Lord." To love the Lord, to consecrate the soul, to seek the life-current in the eternal order of things, to harmonise with the Father's will—all these are one and the same act put in different terms. The same Power that grants the guidance gives help all along the line. There is no other Power on this plane. There are no insuperable obstacles. And whether the stars be favourable or not one may confidently start forth. Experience shows, however, that the external life also tends to respond in due course to these prophecies of the spiritual vision. If we would only permit the word to become flesh in its own way, all would run smoothly, but here is where we are apt to forget, to grow impatient and doubtful.

If the present doctrine be the true one, this method of adjustment or realisation of ideals is very different from the one pursued by those who affirm that man is perfect now. Those who make this assertion condemn the present life and evolution as "appearance." They assert that when man sees himself under the aspect of eternity he sees the true man, all else being illusion. Therefore they reach out in strained, ascetic fervour, and abstractly affirm their perfection. We are viewing the entire subject from a different standpoint. The eternal vision is a picture of what may be. The prophetic forecast shows what may come to me if every day on my European journey I am faithful to the guidance of that day. I do not attain salvation once for all; I work it out daily. I must keep in constant touch with the Spirit, if I would always live by the Spirit. The working out of the eternal vision is in the world of time. The vital question is, Granted the vision of myself as I may be, what shall I do with myself as I am?

We have noted that the fine, poetic rhythms are far within. The leaven is already here, in the heart of the lump. It works from within outwards. I am that ideal now, in a sense, but not objectively. It is resident in me, seeking to come forth. I must then view my outer life in the light of this modification from within. I need not affirm, I need not strain. I ought rather to acquire a keener sense of the law of unfoldment, the "ups and downs," the crests and the depths of the waves, the day and the night, all the details of gradual regeneration.

For example, there is a rhythm of the flesh—the subconscious functioning of all the organs. If I am moderate, poised; if I occasionally rest, learn how to work so as to husband my energy; acquire equanimity, my life becomes so adjusted that I enjoy good health. If I give wise expression to the head and the heart, the instinct for sociability, the prompting to service, I put myself in the divine current in all these respects. For since I am a many-sided being it is rational to assume that many-sided adjustment is required, that there is guidance for each one of these phases of my nature. If my life is to become a divine poem, I must respond to the finer rhythms in each of these departments, I must consciously cultivate beauty.

Think of the divine life-current, then, as flowing out through you, in so far as you are at peace yet active, serving, loving, seeking truth, beauty, and goodness. In every detail, seek not your own ideal or will alone, but ask what the Father would make through you. Reduce all conduct, all life to co-operation with God; cut off all else, simplify life to the finest point. Drop all anxiety, cease all effort to shape things in your own way, trust wholly, at large and in detail. Absorb your consciousness in thought of the ideals resident in all humanity, seeking expression. Dwell upon the positive side. Emphasise the outcome. Do not consider the conditions of evolution alone, but remember the creative rhythms ceaselessly flowing behind and within. Do not be imprisoned in thought of the process, live in joyous thought of its outcome.

Remember that this wonderful subconscious realm in which we dwell is a part of that divine unfolding. When you commit your thoughts and prayers to that realm, you are not delivering them to yourself alone, you are commending them to God. Forth from that realm shall come the guidance needed to lead you to the right environment and the right associates, the solution of the problem that perplexed you, the important letter you wanted to write, the decisive word you longed to utter. The ideas you have read will come forth added to and transfigured. Your scattered thoughts shall be unified, and even your fragmentary doubts shall be turned into unified convictions. All this your subconscious life will do for you, if you trust it, if you give play to its rhythms, if you shape your life in reposeful ways, if you seek symmetry, poise, beauty; if you freely serve and faithfully do the best you know.

The true view of evolution then is from the standpoint of its ideals, and its resources. The universe is an order, a system, springing as a thing of life from the wisdom and love of God. It fulfils many ends, its life flows in many channels. True adjustment takes account of all these by seeking at once the true and the good, the beautiful and the wise, the individual and society; and by seeing all these in God.

Behold your own life in God if you would discover the true clue to its evolution. Return to intimate touch with God, that you may gain a new impetus. Each time you lose hold of your better self, return there again and go forth once more to action. Remember that the fundamental fact is the active presence of God in whose streams of creative tendency your life is immersed and from whom you can draw unlimited life and wisdom and power.

It is impossible to sunder the human mind from the divine life, for consciousness shades off into subconsciousness, and no one can draw a sharp line between the subconsciousness and the divine. Your thought of the true, the beautiful, and the good is not yours alone; it is part of the divine ideal. The less you live for self alone, the more does every thought tend to reflect the beauty of the divine order. Even your imagination may foreshadow coming events, and a score of years hence you may see in actual life that which you once imagined.

We therefore define the soul as precisely such that it can live ever in the current of divine life, yet be in an intimate sense itself. It is futile to try to define the soul apart from these its richest experiences. It is at the same time a resident of eternity and the temporal order, at once the possessor of a conscious and a subconscious mental life. It is fully intelligible only to the degree that we take into account both its profoundest aspirations and its total environment; and the total environment of the soul is, its planes of consciousness, its subconscious life, its communion with God and the world. The world and the soul —that is our life. The world is in part what we call nature, in part our social life, and in part our more direct union with God. The soul is related to nature, it is related to other souls, and it is related to God. Thus the divine order is the true organic unity of all that we experience, the divine will is its centre, the divine love its heart, the divine wisdom the method, and the divine beauty the ideal we seek to realise.

A young minister recently told me an incident in his inner life which admirably illustrates the power of ideals. For weeks he had been greatly overworked, and as a consequence he had been unable to sleep restfully. Among his parishioners there was a man for whom he was deeply concerned, one who was the victim of intemperance. One night before commending his soul to sleep my informant breathed a sort of prayer for light, an earnest appeal for wisdom to aid him in this troublesome case. As he prayed, there occurred to him one of Jesus' most striking sayings, and this Scripture passage was the last thought in his mind before he lost consciousness in sleep. The next morning he awoke feeling much refreshed, after the best sleep during these busy weeks. In his mind, the first thought of the new day was that same Scripture passage, and with it there was still that peculiarly elevating consciousness which the passage suggested.

Aside from the wisdom which may have come from this night of rest in the ideal world, what possibilities of self-development are suggested by this incident! By lifting his thought upward in prayer, by feeling earnest longing, the minister put himself in an ideal attitude. His consciousness was lifted above the level of physical sensation, so that it interposed the least obstacle to the restorative powers of nature. In this attitude he lost consciousness in sleep. The whole night was tempered by this attitude, and the next day was begun with it. The benefits were both physical and spiritual. New inspiration came for the day of service, and a new impetus came into the personal life of the worker.

This incident well illustrates the fact that the absorbing thought of our conscious life gives a dynamic turn to the life of our subconsciousness. Had the last thought been one of bondage to fatigue, the night would probably have been no more restful than those which went before. It does not follow that it is always the last thought which controls the night. But we may safely say that it is the most positive thought. Moreover, there is something peculiarly effective in a thought which lifts the mind. One ascends, as it were, above the clouds, into the pure empyrean. One is detached for the time being from the sweeping tide of anxieties and struggles. If sleep comes at such a moment the entire individual is in the most favourable attitude for " nature's sweet restorer" to do its best. We have barely begun to sound the possibilities in this direction. Consider how much we might accomplish first for ourselves, then for others—when we are fit to labour in their behalf,—by consecrating ourselves afresh each night with some ideal of noble service in mind!

In the first place, this is undoubtedly the most direct way to gain that power which shall restore the tired organism, and put it in better health. For, as we have seen, it is nature that heals. All that any means of regaining health can accomplish, at the utmost, is to remove obstacles to nature's resident power. It is not medicine that heals. Thought does not cure. Nature is competent. Hence, there is every reason to learn how to co-operate with nature. Usually, we accomplish most when we put the mind into an ideal attitude. It is, therefore, of great consequence to know that the mind functions on two levels, that in the ideal region the mind not only interposes no obstacle to nature, but actually draws upon higher sources of power.

But it is not alone in regard to sleep and health that the ideal attitude is effective. It is equally important to put one's self above the clouds for a little time, when the day begins. We may find ourselves immersed in the clouds many times during the day, but the day will be the better because it began well. If we form the habit of seeking the superior world, morning and night, after a time it will be very much easier to ascend to the realm of peace. Possessed of the ability quickly to turn there where all is peaceful, we shall be able at will to transcend our lower mental states many times during the day. In due course we shall live more and more above the clouds in spirit, while working all the better in the lower world with our hands.

This is by no means a new principle. Those who are accustomed to pray night and morning will, perhaps, find what I have said so commonplace that they will wonder why I take space to indulge in truisms, and hence they will miss the point altogether. The point is not the newness but the more detailed knowledge we are gaining in these days in regard to the law, the relation of ideals to the subconscious mind, and above all the relation to health. Many a person moves the lips in prayer who does not lift the soul. Many another prays with a, small segment of the great whole of life without filling the being with the spirit of prayer. Prayer is often restricted to what is called the religious life in a limited sense of the word.

It is desirable to approach the whole subject in a fresh light. The best way to do this is by study of actual life. One incident like the above is worth more than all the arguments in the world. When you have had evidence of the power of ideals, study that evidence to see what it teaches. Call it prayer, suggestion, practical idealism, or what you will, but investigate. You are not half awake to your own resources. A miracle is taking place within you all the time. You are in possession of all the resources you could ever have reason to ask for. Yet you complain of the universe because, as you allege, it has left you helpless.

There is obviously a difference, then, between ignoring a trouble, between neglecting to take proper care of ourselves, and that wise direction of thought which in no way hinders while it most surely helps to remedy our ills. There is strong reason for believing that there is a simple, natural way out of every trouble, that kind Nature, which is another name for the omniscient God, is ever ready to do her utmost for us. We may pass through almost any experience if we realise that the power residing within is equal to the occasion. When we cease to look upon any experience as "too hard," we have made a decided step in wise adjustment to life. Life itself becomes easier and happier when we make this grand discovery, that within each human soul there is a sufficient resource for every need along the line of the individual career. We can conquer anything that lies between us and our individual destiny.

It is also necessary to note the difference between wise adjustment to circumstances which for the time being we cannot alter, and that utter contentment and ease in our surroundings which leads to inactivity and invalidism. Some people are too well adjusted to their environment. They need a sudden stirring, like that sometimes caused by an alarm of fire. They do not grow. They are selfish, and lack even the rudiments of self denial—as though the world existed for their own benefit. Or, perhaps they are self-satisfied, and fail to see the need of further evolution. They are contented, polite and agreeable, so long as nothing comes to disturb them; and they take care that nothing shall disturb them, so far as their power extends. If they are ill, everyone must become a servant. Every sensation is watched and carefully nursed. Everything must give way to their wishes. Everybody must help by expressions of sympathy and devotion. But place such people on their own resources, put them where something does disturb, and they are utterly helpless.

Progress brings conflict. We need to be stirred once in a while, and put where we must show what we are really worth. Then comes the real test. If we are adjusted, not to some transient set of circumstances which we personally try to maintain undisturbed, but to life as a whole so far as we understand it, we shall be able to meet any emergency, meet it manfully, trustfully, contentedly. There is no better test of one's philosophy than at these times, when we are called upon to act as if we believed it true. There is no better way to prepare for such emergencies than to meet the circumstances of daily life as though we were superior to them.

It is a matter of economy, it is a source of happiness to ourselves and our friends, if we habitually look for the good wherever we go, and in this way show our superiority to all that is belittling and mean. We shall soon find no time left for complaint and discouragement if we undertake this happy task with a will. We shall discover new traits of character in our friends, new sources of enjoyment in trivial things, and new pleasures even in the weather—that potent cause of useless complaint and regret. New beauties will reveal themselves in nature and in human life. We shall gradually learn to see life through the artist's eyes, to look for its poetry, its harmony, its divine meaning.

The traveller in foreign lands is compelled to meet experience in such a philosophical mood. He knows that each day is bound to bring its annoyances; and he determines to see their comical side. In a foreign land one makes it an occupation to hunt up all that is curious and interesting. The spirits are quickened, enthusiasm is aroused; and one notices a hundred little effects, changes, and beauties in sky and landscape, on the street and in people, that are passed unnoticed at home. We make note of them in order to describe them to our friends. Imagination lends its charm even to the most disagreeable experiences, and all our journeyings stand out in the vistas of memory painted in golden hues.

Such experiences should give us the cue in looking for the good at home. It is well, too, in matters of disagreement with friends, to preserve the same large spirit and breadth of view, remembering that we have more points of agreement than of disagreement with them, that we all belong to the same infinite Love, and all mean the same great truth; but we cannot quite express it. It is rather better to be tolerant, to have a large charity for people, than to expect them to be like ourselves. One person of a kind is usually enough. God apparently needs us all. Those who have learned to think, especially those who realise the meaning of evolution, are usually aware of their faults; and encouragement is what they most need. People do nearly as well as they can under the circumstances and with their scant wisdom. If we know a better way, it will become evident to them if we practise it. If they offend us or become angry, we have all the more cause for charity and good feeling. We need not suffer in such a case unless we put ourselves on the same plane, and become angry, too. There is no quicker or more smarting rebuke than to receive an affront in silence or in good feeling. There is no better evidence of a large and generous nature than immediately to forgive and to forget every injury, and thereby to be superior to the petty feelings of resentment, pride, and unforgiveness, which work mischief alike to the one who holds them and to the one who has done the injury. We are surely to blame if we suffer, since everything depends on our active attitude.

If we thus give our attention to building character, broad, charitable, and true, the wrong thoughts will disappear through mere lack of attention. Psychology once more helps us here, and shows that we can attend to but one object at a time. Science tells us, too, that in the evolution of the animal world organs which remain unused ultimately disappear, while the development and perfection of an organ accompanies its use. We need not then reason our erroneous thoughts away. Usually, it is sufficient to see that we are in error, to learn that all these fears, resentments, morbid thoughts, and complaints affect our health and happiness. "The explanation is the cure."

Nor is it necessary to analyse sensation or try to discover the various moods that cause our trouble. No one who has passed through the torments of self-consciousness, to find only one's own insignificant self looming up through the introspective mist, like a repellent spectre from which one would fain be free, will ever advise another to brave these torments. The human self with the divine Self as a background is the only picture of the inner life which one can bear to look at long. This picture will paint itself. The other is of our own vain contriving. In those moments of calm reflection when one ceases to analyse self, and puts aside the cares of the busy world, the deeper consciousness will be quickened. One falls into a gentle revery. pleasant memories and past experiences come before the mind. One sees wherein one has failed to practise one's truest wisdom, or sees the meaning of an experience that seemed hard and inexplicable at the time. Then, as one gradually turns in thought from personal experience to the larger experience of humanity in its relation to the great Over-soul, all these varied events and personalities will be regarded in relations unsuspected before. One will have new glimpses of truth,—of the deeper truth which is ever ready to make itself known when one is intuitively awake and receptive.

A synthesis of these spontaneous reflections will give more genuine knowledge of self than any purely introspective process. And likewise in any moment of trouble or sickness, when we need help, it is better to open out like the flower, receptively, quietly, expectantly, conscious of the nearness of the divine Helper, than to pursue our own thought, and try to solve the difficulty. We are too active as a rule, too sure of our own way, too much absorbed in our own plans and fears. The Spirit demands but little of us—quiet, lowly listening—but it does ask this much. Here is the real power and value of silence. All that we perceive in these moments of quiet reflection has a lasting effect upon us. It is then that we grow. It is then that ideals take shape, and become permanent directions of mind. It is then that we become newly adjusted to life; for, after all, this task is never completed. Something new and perplexing is ever coming to test us; and always there is this one resource, to find our inward centre, and there to stand firm and contented.

It is also in these more deeply reflective moments that we learn our own limitations and possibilities. We become aware of that deepest tendency which lies at the basis of temperament and personality, through which the great Spirit speaks. We learn a deeper and truer self-reliance, which ultimately means trust in God. We learn through experience when to obey this inner moving and when the impulse is merely our own personal desire. In a word, conduct reduces itself to one simple rule: Study to know when you are moving along the lines of your own deepest nature, your own keenest sense of what is wise and right, and when you are off the track. It is right and necessary to have certain standards by which conduct may be judged, to have a philosophy which teaches one to look on all sides of an issue and to reason carefully. It is well to look to friends, to public teachers and books, for help in all humility and willingness to learn. But standards vary. The conscience of a people changes from age to age. Even intuition must be empirically verified; it must find support in reason, and undergo the test of experience. The surest and simplest method, for those who have become aware of such guidance, is to await the divine emphasis, to act when the whole being speaks, to move along those lines in which no faculty of one's being interposes an obstacle. All ultimate questions of right and duty should obviously be settled within the sacred limits of one's own personality, where the great God speaketh, if He speaks at all. "The soul's emphasis is always right," says Emerson.

To some this doctrine may seem like mere individualism, urging one, as it does, to find a resource for all trouble in one's own nature. Yet, rightly interpreted, it is by no means selfish; it seeks to give the individual mental freedom and opportunity for development within the limits of what is required of him as a member of society. We have thus far considered the problem of adjustment in its simplest form. All that has been said in the foregoing chapters properly enters into the question—the nature and relationship of the immanent God to His manifestations, and all that we know about those manifestations.

Society is, ideally at least, an organism. Human minds as well as human customs and social institutions are evolving together. One by one, and individual by individual, we are related in one great mental, social, and universal experience. Each need, each aspect of the organism, the adjustment of part to part and of means to ends, demands special consideration, We must, for example, consider and preserve our physical well-being. In this endeavour we are aided by all that science has discovered concerning the human body, its evolution, its care, and the need of exercise. We have duties to our fellow-men in regard to the well-being of society. Duty enters into every department of human life. We owe it to our neighbour, to the universal brotherhood or the divine fatherhood, to be doing something in particular all the time, to choose this line of conduct and reject that. And this knowledge of duty should rest on a scientific interpretation of the universe, on a study of life in its total relations.

No one can think deeply about life without considering these larger issues. But, even in approaching the problem of adjustment in its simpler and more individual aspects, we discover many ways in which we may pay our large debt to society. One cannot develop far beyond the less thoughtful masses without leading them on; and, since man is an imitative creature, there is no surer way of helping him than by setting him a nobler example. Our uncharitable, our fault-finding and fear-carrying words and thoughts are sometimes as harmful to others as to ourselves. When we overcome these wrong habits of thought, our friends will not be slow in noticing the change. With the advent of a habit of looking for the good, of deriving encouragement from everything, and of disposing of our troubles in a quiet way ourselves, instead of burdening others with them, the reaction on our associates will prove wonderfully helpful.

This doctrine, then, says in a word, Be unselfish; have an ideal outlook; see yourself as you would like to be, healthy, happy, well-adjusted to life, helpful, wisely sympathetic, ever ready with an encouraging word, looking for the good, growing strong in wisdom and power; patiently awaiting occasions, yet always sufficiently occupied, so that you will have no time to be annoyed, fearful, restless, or morbid. It points out new ways in which we may be of service to our fellow-men. It makes us aware of our own responsibility, and shows us that life is an individual problem. It warns us never to look upon that problem as too difficult to solve, if we approach it moderately, hopefully, and full of cheer.

Is it not a duty to be supremely happy, forever young in spirit? We have all met people whose very being seems to thrill from some unseen source of happiness. What influence can resist such a power, and what trouble can long weigh down such a bounding spirit? It is like the glad song of the birds, which will not let us be melancholy, or the feeling of worship for the Source of all life, which wells up in the presence of some beautiful landscape. It is health. It opens one to the renewing, the indwelling energy, by which we exist, whereas fear contracts, and causes one to shut out that energy. There is something profoundly unhealthy in our thought if any trouble whatever leads us to suppress this happy tendency. Its source is eternal, its spirit perennial. Its power in counteracting the selfish and morbid tendencies in life is boundless. It is not to be sought for its own sake alone. It is not the end of life. It is rather the spontaneous accompani-ment of the highest usefulness, the deepest worship, the truest love, the greatest thankful-ness, the profoundest repose and trust in God. It is the truest sanity. It marks a well-balanced mind.

Science and philosophy do not always satisfy the soul. Reason sometimes leaves room for doubt. Pessimism and despair often rush in, if we do not check them by some happy thought. The greatest assurance, the one that never fails, is this happy restfulness, which no doubt can shake, this feeling that we are right, this sublime faith which sees no barrier between the soul and its perennial source. A sense of trust and thankfulness wells up with this deep assurance, a feeling of joy in the blessing of existence, which defies the subtlest scrutiny, which unites the simplicity of childhood with the profoundest reaches of manhood's thought. It is well to take note of its conditions when it comes, to observe what a range of thought and sentiment is opened up by genuine happiness, and then, when the spirit of depression weighs heavily upon us, to recall these conditions, to let the morbid thought languish for mere want of attention, to stir one's self, to arouse a forced happiness if one cannot shake off the heavy spirit in any other way.

It is a matter of economy to be happy, to view life and all its conditions from the brightest angle. It enables one to seize life at its best. It calls power to do our bidding. It renews. It awakens. It is a far truer form of sympathy than that mistaken sense of communion with grief and suffering which holds our friends in misery instead of helping them out of it. It is a far nobler religion than that creed which causes one to put on a long face, and look serious. Once more, there is something wrong in our philosophy if it sanctions melancholy and pessimistic thoughts. We have not yet looked deeply enough into life. We are still thinking and acting contrary to, not in harmony with, the happy world of nature by which we are surrounded. By maintaining this mournful attitude, we show our want of faith in the goodness of things as much as when we fear. A deep, unquenchable spirit of joy is at once the truest evidence that we believe in the beneficence of the Father, and that we have penetrated deep enough into life's mystery to see how best, most economically, most courageously and helpfully to take it.

Patience, too, is a word that suggests much that is needful in the adjustment to life. Hard, indeed, is it for some to abide nature's time, hard to eliminate the idea that creation was completed long ago. Consider for a moment the vast age of our fair earth, how many aeons of cosmic time it revolved in space before vegetation appeared, and then pass in imagination down through the long cycles of struggle and development which led the way to the production of the first man, a creature with whom we would not own kinship. History is still young. It is made today with unwonted rapidity, and one can hardly keep pace with the advancing times. Yet nature is just as moderate as ever, and our century is but the bursting bud of ages of measured preparation. Long ago the ancient Greeks spoke for beauty of form. Long ago Jesus spoke for the beauty of service. Not so long ago Luther spoke for freedom of conscience and reason. Slowly the great world is brought round to the perception of these great prophets, who stand like guide-posts, indicating the will of the Most High.

Progress is as measured in human life. We cannot hasten events. We may as well accept the conditions of progress as we find them, and not postpone our lesson. My experience of today is the outcome of my experience of yesterday, of my past life, and is largely conditioned by it. My intuition tells me of grander experiences to come. It gives ideals. But I cannot enjoy those experiences now, I cannot yet realise the ideals, because I cannot omit one step in my progress. I am ready, in the full sense of the word, only for the step which logically follows the one I am just now taking. I must not overreach or work myself into a nervous strain. I must not let my thoughts dwell on the future. I must not be anxious nor assert my own will, for I do so at the peril of my health and happiness. I ought rather to live in the living present, understand my experience in the light of immediate cause and effect. I must build my new future by gradual modification of the changing present. I must select and reject, choose and neglect.

For, despite the fact that this endless chain of causes and effects, whereof my fleeting experience is a part, is law-governed and fate-driven, I have a wonderful amount of freedom. I am able not only to choose between accepting life's conditions trustfully, contentedly, making the most that is good out of them, or rebelliously complaining at them all. I not only make of the world what I put into it, and thus regulate my own happiness and misery; but I cause infinite misery to other people. I may sin, I may degrade myself lower than the animals, I may be thoroughly wicked and mean,—all within certain limits,—I may make of myself what I will; but I can never escape the torments, the inevitable results of my own acts. Not all the creeds, not all the good men, not all the prayers and sacrifices in the world, can ever change natural law, or save me from the heaven or the hell which I am preparing for myself by my daily conduct. What I am doing day by day is resistlessly shaping my future—a future in which there is no expiation except through my own better conduct. No one can save me. No one can live my life for me. It is mine for better or for worse. If I am wise, I shall begin today by the simplest and most natural of all processes to readjust my conduct. As surely as the great world of human thought comes round to the position of one wise man, so surely does the whole fabric of personal thought and action respond to our will. We have only to wait, be patient, renew our ideals day by day, remember that ideas have regenerative life and a natural law of growth, then act.

Here, then, is the secret of the whole matter. To look persistently toward the light, toward the good, toward what we would rather be, and as we would rather feel when we are suffering, with some happy prospect in view if we are morbid, with some deed of kindness in mind if we are idle and in need of something which shall absorb and fix the attention. Such will-power as this is irresistible. It is the God and one that make a majority.

Adjustment to life, then, is an individual problem, and varies with temperament, surroundings, and habits of thought. Its principles are universal. First, to realise in our own way the truth of Chapter II., that we live with God; that God lives in us; that He is completing us, moving upon us through the forces, the events, the world in which He resides, through our weaker nature, through our faults, through the conflicts which we have so long misinterpreted, through pain, through happiness, and all that constitutes experience; that we have no power wholly our own, but that we use and are used by divine power; that we are equal to any task, any emergency, any struggle, for God is here. Help is near. We need not go anywhere for it. It is omnipresent. It abounds. It comes to us in proportion to our receptivity to it, our faith in it, our happiness, our hope, our patience. Then to choose wisely what we wish to be in co-operation with the immanent Life, since "whatever determines attention determines action"; to see one's self not in the introspective, but in the divine light; to be practical in the choice of ideals; to be ever happy, ever young, ever hopeful, and never discouraged.

But can we practise all this? If we could apply the entire doctrine at once, it would be of little value. We must have ideals—ideals which we may begin to realise today; and our discussion has been of some use, if it has shown the necessity of moderation, of quiet, trustful imitation of the methods whereby the great world of nature has come into being.

Everyone who has dwelt for a season in that joyous world of the larger hope, where one is lifted above self, above the thought of space and time, so that one seems related to the revolving orbs of space and to the limitless forces of the universe, knows that there is a sudden, almost painful descent to the realities of everyday life. Life is a constant readjustment. It requires a daily renewal of one's faith, and then a return to the tasks, the struggles, which at times well-nigh weigh us down. It means repeated failure. It means a thorough test of all that is in us. It often means trouble and discouragement whenever one receives new light and regenerative ideas, since a period of darkness similar to the decay of the seed in the ground follows every incoming of greater power. But it is priceless knowledge to know that we are equal to the occasion. It is a long step toward self-understanding when we learn to see in facts that once caused discouragement profound reasons for hope and cheer. It is a decided step toward self-mastery when we learn to meet these "ups and downs," these regenerative periods, in a broadly philosophical spirit, at once superior to our circumstances and to the thoughts and fears which once held us in their power. It is fortunate, indeed, if we no longer deem life's task too hard, if our faith be sufficiently strong to sustain us through the severest tests, thereby proving our fitness to be made better, our willingness to persist, though all be dark, with an iron determination to succeed.

Chapter XI
Poise

—

WE are now in a position more definitely to consider the wise attitude by which man may adapt himself to the tendencies of spiritual evolution. For we have seen that the habitual attitude is the determining factor. In the end it is our mode of life that counts. Hence the further we penetrate into the ideal region the more empirical must be our pursuit. Others may indeed give us the benefit of practical experience, but it is individual experiment that makes clear the reality. Ideals are of incalculable assistance, but the ideal differs with every individual. Hence one must take the present discussion as suggestive rather than adequate. The essential is for each man to come to consciousness of the point attained in evolution, and begin with the opportunities immediately at hand.

The question, What is the ultimate ideal? proves in the light of our investigation to be a large problem for one individual to consider. To some people, the universe is instinct with purpose. Others see no reason in an argument for a world-plan. To some it seems impossible that the world could have been better than it is. Others hold that life could not have been worse. All conclusions and all ideals are relative to the state of development. Yet for all men life is some sort of adjustment between inner and outer conditions. To discover that life moves forward and each of us suffers or rejoices according to our dynamic relation to it is perhaps the chief need. And probably the majority of men would agree that the highest aim of life is the full development of the soul. It is character that avails. If we are cast about by every wind that blows it is because we lack the repose that character brings. And to possess character is in some degree to possess one's soul.

Hence it is not out of place to ask, What is the soul? How difficult it is to answer except in empirical terms! One may as well undertake to state what God is apart from His world, as to define the soul apart from what we have felt and thought and willed. Yet we know fairly well what we mean by the term "soul" until we are asked to define it; and we have some conception of the ideal realm of thought, where dwell the poets and philosophers who speak words of comfort to the soul. Our own deepest reflection transports us there, and we seem larger as a result of our meditation. There are experiences that call us out of and above ourselves, noticeably those that make us acquainted with grief in its larger sense; and the soul seems to grow with the new experience. We know when, on the one hand, a man's soul speaks through his words, and when, on the other, he says one thing with his lips and thinks another, thereby trying to conceal his soul. The whole being speaks through a perfectly genuine act, through truly ethical conduct. We mean something genuine, something honest, appealing, and true, bespeaking that indefinable thing called "personality." It is a part of what we call " temperament." It is that which endears one to those who give us a glimpse of God, and makes one feel assured that life, since it produces such a thing as this, is well worth all its hardships. It is the test of all that is dearest and truest in human experience. It is that which transcends, yet gives unity to the intellectual and moral man. Through it comes that wisdom which leads men to act better than they know, which bids one be calm when there is seemingly reason to fear and grieve, which assures one that all will be well even when one feels profound doubts. It is the meeting-point of the eternal Spirit with the ever-varying experiences of daily life.

Our deepest life, then, is a continuous incoming of renewing, sustaining power welling up from the heart of the universe into the spirit of man, a continuous, divine communication engaged in the rearing of a soul. The deepest self is not physical, nor even intellectual; it is spiritual. We are spirits now, in germ it may be; but, in so far as we are conscious of our life with God, that consciousness will probably never be broken. Man is not a body with a soul, but a soul or spirit, which in every well-poised person is master of the body and of the powers of thought and action.

If the soul is in reality uppermost in importance, it is our duty to keep the consciousness of the soul supreme. Many people work so hard at their vocations that their souls have no room to grow. They are lawyers, doctors, financiers, with whom business stands first, not men in the spiritual sense of the word. Anything which subordinates the soul, and prevents man from taking all that belongs to him as a free spirit in a beneficent world, any mistaken sense of humility or self-suppression, has a harmful effect on the whole life, and is evidently as far from a normal attitude as strong self-conceit. If one constantly feels promptings to do good, and suppresses them, a reaction is sure to follow. It is better to express the impulse, even in a slight way, if one cannot realise one's deepest and fullest desire. Theological creeds often suppress the soul. One feels a desire to be larger, freer, and to think for one's self. Want of charity, continued fault-finding, the attempt to do a task that is beneath one, narrows the soul. Love, of the truer sort, broad thinking, open-heartedness, happiness develops it. Sacrifice of individuality to the control of a stronger mind suppresses the soul. Mis-directed education often crushes out originality.

It is well, therefore, to consider wherein we are held down by people and circumstances, and to discover how we are cramping our souls. The soul should be master, and the powers of thought and activity should be free. Do we not yield part of our manhood or womanhood when we worry, when we give way to continued grief or discouragement? On the other hand, is not the realisation of what we are as living, growing spirits, who use the body as an instrument, and control it by thought, who dwell with God and need never fear any permanent harm—is not this the way to free ourselves most rapidly from all that would hold us down?

We have all experienced those calmer moments when we quietly faced our fears, our doubts, and our wavering opinions, and as calmly dismissed them, henceforth powerless because we saw their utter absurdity. Half the battle is won when we discover our error, and realise the possibilities of the soul. We are momentarily masters of the situation. We are more truly and profoundly ourselves, we discover our inner centre, and become poised, grounded in eternal reason and calm in eternal peace. This is at once the highest use of the will and the truest spiritual self-possession; for it is in these moments of calm decision, when we realise our relationship to eternal power, that the mind changes, and brings all things round to correspond to our deep desire. The ideal of daily conduct is to maintain this inward repose, to keep it steadily and persistently in view, to regain it when we lose it, to seek it when we need help, to have a calm centre within which is never disturbed, come what may,—a never-yielding citadel of the higher self.

It is evident, then, that all that we have considered in the foregoing chapters, may be restated with deeper meaning in terms of the soul, of spiritual experience. The soul must learn what it is and why it is here. It must gain this knowledge by actual experience, in order to learn the value of right conduct, in order to learn that there is an immanent Wisdom, a Love, that is equal to all occasions. It must descend into density, or matter, and become acquainted with darkness, in order to discover the meaning of life and become conscious of itself as an individualisation of God. It struggles upward and forward to completion. It is ever trying to come forth and express itself; and, when man comes to consciousness of what it means to develop the soul, and of the divine trend in his personal life, he no longer resists this deep moving. He comes to judgment, and sees how he might have acted more wisely. With this deeper consciousness comes readjustment to life and more spiritual freedom. His soul finds better expression through the body, not in some future existence or in another body, but here and now; for even its experiences in the flesh are soul experiences, and demand, not punishment in the flesh at some distant time, but better and truer conduct in the present.

If anything is purposeful in the universe, then, it is the life, the aspiration and character, the soul of man, as it passes from stage to stage in its progressive experience, unfolding and giving to the light the divinity involved in its very being. It is the knowledge of this permanent factor in so much that is passing and trivial which gives poise and strength to pass through any experience without fear that it may prove too hard.

People disturb us. They narrate their troubles and describe their sensations with painful minuteness of detail. Crowds, city rush and noise, deprive us of our peace. Be as watchful as we may, we find ourselves going off on tangents, on tirades of fear, or on a round of gloomy thoughts. We are misunderstood, ill-used, and wronged. Our faith is tested to the utmost, and we are pushed to the wall. There is obviously but one wise course to pursue in all such cases, namely, not to be disturbed, not to enter into the painful narration, not to rush with the crowd or countenance gloomy thoughts; not to feel uncharitable, revengeful, or unforgiving—since one will only add more trouble—but to regain one's poise by the realisation of the Power that is ever with us. Find your centre, learn to know your home in God, and you can safely let the great world go on, and let nature right all wrongs and heal all hurts.

I need hardly remind the reader that it is not so-called will power that invites this repose, but the higher and truer will explained in the foregoing chapters; for self-assertion defeats one's object. People who are strong in themselves alone obviously have no poise in this deeper sense, as a soul-experience. Those who reach out after the ideal as though it were somewhere afar off and not immanent in the real, who look forward to the future with a nervous strain instead of living in the present, where help is alone to be found, lose what little poise they have, and fly aloft in a burst of enthusiasm. Consciousness is concentrated wherever we send our thought; and, if we reach out or pray to God as a distant being, the thought is sent away from its proper sphere. It were better not to have ideals at all than to strain after them, and assert that they shall become facts at once; for nature's method of measured transformation through evolution is the only wise and health-giving course to pursue.

To know that everything we need is within, here and now, this is poise. Realisation, not assertion, is the method of this book,—a realisation which teaches through actual communion with it that there is an omnipresent Spirit to whom we may turn at any moment and in any place, of whom our being partakes, who is so near to us that we have no wisdom, no power, no life wholly our own.

We are so accustomed to think of the divine nature as wholly unlike and separated from our own character that it is long before we can make this realisation a power in daily consciousness. We have taken credit to ourselves for qualities which inhere in the Essence itself. We have limited our worship of God to one day in the week, to one place of prayer, and sought His revelation in one Book. Dogmas have crystallised about us, and we have hardly dared to think for ourselves. Yet a little reflection shows that we are, that we must be, partakers of the omnipresent Love; that not the Bible alone or any other sacred book, but every book through which the soul of its author speaks untrammelled, all that spurs man on to progress, is a revelation of God, for He is not an exclusive, but an inclusive God. This being so, we obviously do not know ourselves, do not possess ourselves, and have no permanent centre of repose, until we discover the inward kingdom of heaven.

We then learn that there is something within that will teach man better than any mere thought of his own, that he has a wellspring of guidance and inspiration in his own soul. It gives quietness and comfort to know this fact. Nearly everyone has had such guidance at times, sudden warnings of approaching danger and impressions not to do this or that; and help has often come to us during sleep. But this realisation of the nearness of the Spirit gives a reason for such experiences, and encourages one to believe that they can be cultivated and relied on. Then, too, it gives one confidence and strength of a truer sort, not in self-consciousness, and the products of one's own intellectual development, but in that larger Self which is ordinarily crowded out of mind by sentiments of pride and self-satisfaction. One loses fear, one ceases to worry about one's friends or to suffer for wrongs that one is powerless to prevent, when this realisation becomes a habit; for, if God, and not man, is behind events, we can safely trust the universe to Him, and not only the universe, but our friends, our suffering and ignorant fellow-beings, and our own souls. The sense of officiousness is displaced by a feeling of patient trustfulness, and we spare ourselves a deal of unnecessary suffering.

Education of the truer sort brings poise; for it develops individuality, health, and strength of intellect, which in turn aids in the attainment of health and strength of body. Physical exercise, music, or any line of work which rounds out the character and acts as a balance-wheel, is essential for the same reason, since it draws the activities out of narrow and therefore unhealthy directions of mind. Those who are intense in disposition often find it necessary to exercise vigorously, in order to counteract this extreme mental activity, until by degrees they become less and less intense, and learn to work moderately and easily. There is an easiest, simplest way of doing everything, with the least degree of strain and nervous anxiety. We do not learn it while we hold ourselves with the grip of will-power, when we try to work our brains, and force the activities into a given channel. "Self-possession forgets all about the body when it is using it." It interposes no obstacle to the physical and mental forces. It discovers the easiest method of concentration through inward repose, and finds in this quiet restfulness the greatest protection from nervous reaction and fear.

Poise, then, is an affair of degrees. Many have it on the physical plane, and are apparently seldom disturbed in their physical life. Systematic physical exercise brings control of the muscles of the body, and with this control comes a certain degree of poise. In learning to play a musical instrument, one gains it through long training; and we say of a great musician that he has repose, that he plays or sings without effort. But one may have bodily repose, yet have no repose of character, and may be the victim of a veritable whirlwind of nervous excitement within. Those who are aware of their own mental development and soul growth are usually conscious of touching a deeper and deeper centre, and with each experience comes added poise and readjustment to life. Every trying experience demands a strengthening of one's faith, a deepening of one's self-possession; for the natural tendency is to fear, worry, and doubt. We are not sure of ourselves until we have undergone the test of severe experience. Any experience, then, that strengthens this inward repose is rather a blessing than a hardship. Is it too much to say that we may become equal to any experience whatever, and meet it unmoved within, in quiet trust and perfect faith? Surely, the possibility is worthy of consideration.

If we have proved to our satisfaction that two and two make four, and that the result will always be the same, we are undisturbed by those who affirm that the result should be five. So far as we have rationalised experience and discovered certain laws, our conviction is no less certain, because nature, like mathematics, is a system on which we may rely. If the reader is convinced that God is immanent, or that evolution, so far as science has described it, is a true statement of life's process of becoming, this knowledge furnishes a basis on which to reason. It gives poise and inspires trust. To be sure, the conditions may change, and other forces counteract and modify the results in a given case. To the forgetfulness of this fact is due the tenacity with which some people cling to their beliefs, simply because they are unaware of these modifying circumstances and causes.

If the reader has grasped the few great but highly important laws of human life, he is now able to rise superior to moods, troubles and illnesses, which once would have caused great suffering. Simply to know that every event has an adequate cause, that action and reaction are equal, that experience depends on our attitude towards it, and that with a change of mind, a new directing of the will, the forces of our being are brought round to correspond, this simple knowledge is enough to give us poise, and make us masters.

One's method of adjustment to life or one's optimism need not, let us repeat, be identical with the teaching of this book.* There are as many lines of approaches as there are temperaments; and that is precisely the point of this chapter. Have a method. Have a soul of your own. Be your self. Think, realise, until you have a measure of unborrowed conviction, which establishes a centre of repose, and is a source of happiness and contentment, a centre which yields to no outer tumult, but is receptive to the Spirit; which never harbours fear or doubt, no matter what the wavering self may say; which never wavers, never forgets that the individual belongs to the Universal, never relaxes its hold of that which is deepest, truest, most spiritual in life, come what may, be it sorrow, illness, or any calamity which life may bring; a centre which rests at last on the love of God. And, when you lose this poise, regain it, as though you would say, "Sit still, my soul: thou at least must not lose thy composure nor thy awareness of the eternal presence of God."

Hence the present inquiry should be supplemented by the poetic and religious literature which most strongly appeals to the reader, by further studies in the life of the soul, by references to Emerson, Amiel, Maeterlinck and other essayists who have interpreted the inner life.

Those who are nervously inclined will find it necessary to stop themselves many times a day when they discover that they are under too great pressure. They will find themselves hurrying unnecessarily or becoming inwardly excited. Oftentimes all that is needed in order to prevent serious mental and physical trouble is to take off this pressure, and find this quiet inward centre. It is wonderfully refreshing and removes fatigue to relieve the pressure. Simply to turn away from self, and all that destroys repose, to the Self which knows the supreme peace, is sufficient to give help and strength at any time and in any place. The wise direction of mind opens the door to help. If we trust, if we expect it, the help will come, whereas the nervous effort to compel it to come will put an obstacle in its pathway.

To know how to rest, this is the great need of our hurrying age. We are too intense, too active. We have not yet learned the power and supremacy of the Spirit, nor the value of quiet, systematic thinking. We struggle after ideas. We read this book and that, and go about from place to place in search of the latest and most popular lecturer, instead of pausing to make our own the few great but profoundly simple laws and truths of the Spirit. We are unaware of the power and value of a few moments of silence.

Yet it is in our periods of receptivity that we grow. Not while we actively pursue our ideas do we obtain the greatest light. Oftentimes, if the way is dark, and we can find no help, it is better to cease striving, and let the thoughts come as they may, let the Power have us; for there is a divine tendency in events, a tendency in our lives which we may fall back on, which will guide us better than we know, if we listen, laying aside all intensity of thought, and letting the activities settle down to a quieter basis.

Here is the vital thought of this book, its most urgent appeal to suffering humanity and the soul in need. Part of its teaching can only be verified by experience, and must seem merely theoretical to many readers. But here is a thought that is for everyone, a simple, practical thought, that leads to and includes all the rest. Let us pause for a time, think slowly and quietly, and not leave it until we have made it our own.

Wise silence invites the greatest power in the world, the supreme Power, the omnipresent Life. Let us be still in the truest and deepest sense of the word, and feel that Power. It is the Spirit in all things. It surrounds us here and now, in this present life, this beautiful world of nature, of law and order, this inner world of thought and the soul. It is supreme wisdom and perfect love. It knows no opposition. There is naught to disturb its harmonious, measured, and peaceful activity. It is beauty and peace itself. Its love and peace are present here with us. Let us then be still. Peace, peace, there is nothing to fear. In this restful happy moment we have won the peace of eternity, and it is ours forever.

Who that has communed with the Power of silence in this way can do justice to the unspeakable joy of that moment of rest and peace? It is not suggestion alone that brings it. It is something more than mere thought. The experience is one of deep, inner stillness. The receptivity of the soul invites the supreme Love itself, the eternal Peace. Hence the soul's attitude is all-important. At best, any formula of thought or mental picture is a superficial aid.

Many will find it difficult at first to banish other thoughts; and it is better not to force the stillness to come, but to let the agitation cease by degrees, letting the thoughts come until they quiet down for mere want of conscious attention. When at last the attention no longer wanders here and there, but is poised in the present moment, and the feeling of peace becomes uppermost, it is better to cease definite thought altogether, and simply enjoy the silence. One will then have a sense of incoming power and of newness of life which no other experience can bring. This may not be the result at first, since it is only after repeated trials that one learns how to become still. One may even be made more nervous by the simple thought of stillness. It is often easier to realise this peace for another than for one's self, but the result will in time be the same. The consciousness will be drawn away from self and physical sensation; and this, after all, is the essential—to rise above self into the nobler world of altruism and the Spirit.

Some have found it helpful to set aside fifteen minutes each day for quiet receptivity of this deeper sort. Then, when times of trouble and suffering come, one will not lose one's self-possession, but will know how and where to find help.

The instance is related of a student in the university of Leipzig who was in such an intense state of nervous strain that the students and professors were much alarmed at his condition. As the result of good advice he took up the habit of sitting quietly by himself for about fifteen minutes each day, in absolute silence, maintaining as nearly as possible a state of perfect composure and muscular rest, banishing all thought and all activity. In a short time he made a very noticeable improvement, and finally recovered his health. The mere effort of maintaining an easy, relaxed state of mind and body had relieved him of the inner pressure.*

Of course some readers will explain such cases in purely physiological terms. But it is more important to dwell upon the spiritual values than either the physiological or the psychical data.

If one fails utterly at first to gain this silent repose, and becomes still more restless, one should not be discouraged. That is the moment to rejoice and to know that one has in part succeeded. The experience is the same in all efforts of reform. The first result is to stir up and encounter opposition.

Suppose for a moment that the reader is impatient, and, seeing the error of his ways, decides to exercise self-control. Very likely he will lose his patience on the first occasion, and act or speak impulsively. Discouragement naturally follows; and the reader forgets one of the great laws of growth,—the law, namely, that a period of darkness, of regeneration, of sharp contact with all that can rouse itself into opposition, follows the reception of new light, of greater power. Conservatism and habit are ever ready to rise and say that there shall be no reform. All healthy changes are evolutionary, not revolutionary. We forget that an idea, like a seed, has life, and, if sown in the mind, will grow. We forget the outcome. We often falsely accuse ourselves of sin, when the relapse is really due to a firm determination to be better. If we keep the end in view, if we have an ideal outlook, we may let the disturbance be what it may. Quiet persistence is the word. Each effort to renew our ideal adds to its evolutionary power. " Keep your eye fixed on the eternal, and your intellect will grow," says Emerson.

One's first real success in attaining this inner repose sometimes comes alone with nature when, standing in silence under the pines and thinking in harmony with their whispering or awed by some grand mountain scene, one freely and fully yields to the spirit, the calm, the rhythm of one's surroundings. Afterwards one may return in thought to the mountain summit, where the eternal silence of the upper air was so deeply impressive. Or one may imagine one's self by the sea, where the ceaseless ebb and flow of the surf on a sandy shore once quieted the troubled spirit; or afloat at sea on a beautiful June day, listening to the regular play of the waves along the steamer's side. Any thought which suggests silence will produce the result, until one acquires the habit of thinking in harmony with the rhythm of nature.

Everything in nature seems to have its ebb and flow, its alternation of day and night, of activity and rest, the one blending with the other throughout the seasons and the centuries. The strains of a grand symphony carry one in thought to this region of rhythmic alternation. One is glad enough at times to lay aside present problems and everything that is modern, and read the great authors who wrote for all time, or read some history or scientific work which transports one to the past, and gives one a sense of time, of the long ages and the periods through which the earth has passed and man has worked his way.

There seems to be a corresponding rhythm in human life, with its joys and sorrows, its successes and its failures. Yet the interval is often too long for our short-sighted discernment. In the night of trouble and despair we forget that the day will surely dawn again. We occasionally emerge into remembrance of what it all means, and we think that now at last all will go well. Then comes the descent. We are plunged once more into the depths, where the facts of life are seen at the close, pessimistic range; and once more our memory fails to hold over. But in due time these contrasted experiences fall into a system, if we reflect on their meaning. We are awed by the eternal fitness of things. A stronger hand and a profounder will than our own is revealed in the life of our soul.

It is true we make many relative mistakes. Within certain limits we seem to have infinite choice. We are conscious of wrong-doing and we have much to regret. Yet a time comes when many of these experiences yield their meaning. We justify mistakes in the light of their outcome. Each hour of conflict had its place in teaching part of life's great lesson. A world of truth flashes upon us through the memory of some wrong act; and we question the wisdom of the slightest regret, since we have acted so much better than we knew. This soul-experience, this personal evidence that we have been guided, is for many the strongest assurance that our world-order is the best possible order. They are conscious of being led to certain lines of conduct at what they call "the right moment." They see their humble place in the world, and await the next step in quiet expectancy. One may as well tell them they have no eyes as to deny this inward guidance, for it leads them from task to task with a certain system. If it does not tell them what to do, it at least opposes no obstacle. One cannot hasten it. One cannot always discern the proper course until the proper moment. It often comes unexpectedly, causing humility and surprise that so much should be given. But the right thought comes in the fitness of time to those who quietly await it.

Thus one is drawn at last out of the narrow prison of self-consciousness into the larger thought of the whole. It gives rest and trust to feel one's self part of an organism so wonderfully and systematically adjusted, where the world tendency is not alone concerned with the selfish needs of one man, nor the wrongs which one would like to see swept away because we do not see their meaning, but with the total needs of all as related to the total universe.

One loses all sense of time and space under the power of this thought of the wholeness which shades off into eternity. This transient thought of ours, this divine moment of time, is a part of that eternity. It links the limitless future with the irrevocable past. It is as important, as truly a part of eternity, as any moment could ever be. We learn that we are in eternity now, not that it is to come. We try to comprehend what it means—in eternity now, in infinite time, in boundless space, or, better, above all time and space, where one Power, one law, holds all events together, where each and all are inseparably related to the Supreme Reality.

If we dwell in eternity, why need we hurry in soul, whatever bodily hurry may be required? Why should we not dwell here in the everlasting present, instead of reaching off somewhere in thought, anticipating the future and death, as though there would ever be a break in the stream of life? If we, as souls, dwell in eternity, is not our life continuous?

In some of us has been born a desire to live forever. It is probable that we are no more responsible for that desire than for our deepest faith in God. In the supremest moments of human life it is He who stands by us, not we by our faith in Him, and we would fain doubt Him if we could; but we never quite persuade ourselves that He will fail to fulfil every earnest desire and justify all the conditions in which we have been placed, though it take forever. There are times when we seem to dwell in a region where all is good and wise and true; for we have momentary glimpses of the sublime wholeness of things, the sublime reason, the sublime end, a region where, if we have not all power, we at least have as much as we can make our own, and a faith that knows no doubt.

If I display goodness towards another, I partake of the nature of God in some degree. The Love of God speaks through the heart of the mother. It must be a part of the infinite love, since we all belong to Him. Human nature, however individual in its history, is at each moment in some measure dependent on the Supreme Spirit. One's soul is not one's self alone. It is also God's emphasis of some phase of His own nature, the attention of God fixed on some object. One's unquenchable faith is ultimately God's unfailing love. We believe in Him because He knows us, because He possesses us, you and me, and uses, has need of us, because He has made us aware of His presence. He loves us and we trust Him because we must.

This realisation of our relationship with the unthinkably great and eternal, which brings us as near to it and makes us as much part of it here and now in this present moment as though we were this great wholeness, and had lived from all time, is strengthened by considering our indebtedness to the world. Here we are in this beautiful, beautiful world. How wonderfully it is wrought! How systematically it has evolved, governed by exact laws and animated by unvarying forces! It is our home. We may rely upon it and on that heaven-taught instinct which guides its creatures better than the combined wisdom of all mankind. What a delight to exist! What exceptional pleasures come to us at times among the mountains, by the winding streams, the peaceful valleys, the great ocean, inspiring awe alike in storm and calm, and ever suggestive of that Father for whom we all exist, whose love unites us all! Days are continually recurring which stand out above many others because of some charming scene in nature, some impressive communion with the spirit of the woods or the hills, while the dreariest day in winter or the most barren landscape in nature will yield its gift of beauty if we seek it. The poet and the artist see all this, and live in a diviner world because they are watchful. But the beauty is there for all, to inspire contentment if we need it, to reveal the good if we look for it, and to make us thankful and trustful when we consider its deep significance, its correspondence to the beauty of law and order, of need and supply in the inner life.

Then, too, the beauty of human character more than all else endears one to life, and gives one joy in existence. Where one's friends are is one's home, and where they are is always happiness and contentment. One is constantly touched by little acts of kindness and devotion. Sometimes in the country, especially among a simple folk, one draws very near to the heart of humanity. One is moved beyond words, for nothing conceals the honest hearts that reach out to one in all their native feeling and sincerity. Such experiences have a wonderful effect upon the recipient when put beside the darker aspects of life—with those undeniable evidences of wickedness which might otherwise almost persuade one that human life is corrupt to the core.

Omit these darker experiences we cannot in trying to cast our thought into some sort of system; but in daily life we are too inclined to dwell on them, especially to enlarge upon our woes. We are apt to contemplate these darker facts, and never pass beyond them. We stay in gloomy surroundings, and then call the world "ugly." It is well once in a while to pass in review all that should cause us joy and thankfulness, to ascend the mountain of thought, whence we may look beyond the ugly spots and see their relation—and, after all, it is a beautiful one—to the great landscape beyond.

I do not speak alone as one who has stood on the mountain top, and thought the world beautiful, but as one who has suffered keenly and critically in the darksome vales below, who has met with the severest losses and suffered the deepest disappointments, and has had an intense disposition to overcome. Our poise is worth little if it fails to give strength and composure in any possible experience, and to be itself strengthened by the newest trial. The experiences and realisations suggested in this chapter prepare the way for the severer tests of actual life. If we habitually realise what it means to dwell with God, what the soul is, and how it is approaching complete realisation, and keep the ideal of adjustment to life ever before us, pausing in silent receptivity whenever we become too intense, then into the mind will steal the renewing and strengthening Power, which will prepare us for the day of sorrow and the hour of supreme suffering.

Chapter XII
Self-Help

—

WE have now considered the general attitude toward life whereby the vital truths of the inner life may become concrete in daily experience. We have found that attitude to consist in the recognition of what man is as a progressive being, and in wise co-operation with the indwelling Life which resistlessly carries him forward to completion. There is a tendency which will carry man onward if he will acknowledge it. It will guide him in every detail of life, it will help him in every moment of trouble. It is with all men, it is used by all men; for otherwise they could not exist. But to the majority it is unknown and unrecognised, and to assure them that they can have such guidance seems to them the merest folly. To know it, and to distinguish between the merely personal thought or inclination and this diviner moving, is to live the higher life,—a life which proves to be infinitely better and happier as soon as one makes this most helpful discrimination. To turn to it in times of doubt and trouble is to regain one's poise, to become adjusted to life, to gain the truest self-help.

Ordinarily, it is sufficient to maintain this attitude of adjustment and poise, and preserve an ever-deepening consciousness of our life with the Father. Contaminating influences cannot then touch us, fear will have no power over us, we shall respect this inner tendency rather than the opinions of men, and escape a large proportion of the ills which neither the mind nor the flesh is heir to. This realisation will add a meaning, a depth and beauty to life, which the reader who has not yet made it a factor in daily experience can hardly imagine. Simply to discover that so much depends on our mental attitude is of itself sufficient to work a wonderful change in the lives of those who bear this great truth in mind; for, if we begin life afresh, with a determination to see the real meaning and spirit of things, it will be impossible for old habits of thought, fears and inherited notions to win their way into consciousness. The road to better health, to unhoped-for happiness and freedom, is open before us.

There are times, however, when one needs more detailed knowledge of the foregoing principles. The habitual attitude is, as it were, the basis of conduct, but one must also know how to act upon that foundation. Hence it is important to give attention to certain specific problems. A leading clue to this detailed knowledge is found in the fact that in general the emotional life is divided into two types. Fear, jealousy, anger, and all selfish emotions have a tendency to draw the consciousness into self, to shut in and restrict the activities, impede the natural life and restorative power of the body, and develop a condition from which, if it be long maintained, nature can free us only by a violent reaction; whereas a pleasurable emotion, such as one feels when listening to a familiar melody or the strains of a great symphony, causes the whole organism to expand, and sends a thrill to the utmost extremities of the being.

There is a whole vocabulary of words in common use expressing the warmth and coldness of human beings. In fact, the head and the heart, are often taken as types of these fundamental characteristics; and we speak of this church as "cold and intellectual," that one as "warm and spiritual."

Again, considering emotion alone, we speak of warm-heartedness. It seems to be out-going, expansive; and, if one give to another or do an act of kindness, that act has a tendency to repeat itself. The person is touched on whom the favour is conferred, and immediately feels a desire to reciprocate, to show kindness to another. On the contrary, let the emotion be selfish, let the person do a mean act, and there is an instant withdrawing, a narrowing of the soul. Happiness, joy, genuine pleasure, and self-denial are expansive emotions, and oftentimes wonderfully "catching." With the one emotion comes self-forgetfulness and lack of restraint; with the other comes self-consciousness and painful awareness of sensation. Love is warm; selfishness is cold. Happiness expands; fear contracts.

Thus we might pass in review the whole category of human emotions; and, if we could trace their physical effect on the minuter portions of the body, we might discover that the particles are either drawn together or thrown apart by each emotion. When the shock is too great, whether the emotion be one of joy or sorrow, death results, There is evidently, then, a state of equilibrium where, on the one side, the body is harmoniously adjusted and free from restrictions; and where, on the other, the mind is also in adjustment or repose.

This emotional effect, with its accompanying physical changes, may be further illustrated by the sudden and marvellous cures which have taken place in all ages, and are occurring today. It is a well-known fact that these wonderful cures usually occur either among people of strong faith or among ignorant and superstitious—in other words. highly emotional—people. The alleged cures performed through the agency of sacred relies, at holy shrines, at Lourdes, and other well-known wonder-working centres, are wrought almost wholly among strongly superstitious people, who are ready to accept certain beliefs with all the energy of their being.

It is a truism today to affirm that miracles are impossible. The whole fabric of nineteenth century science rests on the knowledge that law is universal. If then, such cures occur—and they are too widely attested to doubt them—they must take place in accordance with a certain principle. This principle is evidently the one already suggested; namely, that the bodily condition changes when the emotions are touched,—not only in sudden cures, but in all that constitutes the emotional life.

The stronger the emotion, other things being equal, the more remarkable the effect or cure. Emotion of a certain sort—noticeably, expectant attention accompanied by implicit faith on the part of an invalid before a sacred relic—has a wonderfully expansive and liberating effect on the body. The entire attention is concentrated on what is about to occur; the thought is lifted above self by the emotional experience; and the physical forces are no longer hampered by fear, morbid awareness of sensation, and the thousand and one feelings which interfere with the natural restorative power of the body. The emotion frees, "opens" the body; density is broken up; and a process of change which ordinarily would require many weeks or months is completed in a short time.

Here, then, is an important fact underlying the entire process of self-help: a change for the better results when the emotions are touched, when some thought or feeling penetrates to the centre, causing an expansion. Something must quicken the activities and rouse the individual to new life. Bed-ridden invalids and lame people have been known to rush out of burning buildings, or forget themselves in their eagerness to rescue a person in danger, completely recovering their health through the sudden change. in other cases, where the patient is selfish in disposition, the chief task is to find some way in which the person shall begin to live for other people, some interest which shall take the thought out of self, and open the organism to the healing power. Whatever be the method employed—the use of physical remedies, prayer, foreign travel—anything that arouses the confidence, the affection, the interest, or even the credulity of the sufferer, will produce the same result. On the other hand, any remedial means which fails to move or touch the centre is of little efficacy. The problem, then, is to discover the method whereby the individual shall most quickly and easily be touched, so that the healing power shall have full and immediate access to the troubled region.

But what causes the emotional change? Why is it that so many people who receive no benefit from medicine are cured by forgetting self and becoming absorbed in some benevolent work? If ignorant and superstitious people can be cured quickly because they are credulous, is there not some deeper law which governs all cases, by the discovery of which the intelligent man may be cured as quickly as the superstitious?

It is clearly the changed direction of mind, resulting in changed action, that brings about the result. Before the sudden cure can result, there must be faith, expectant attention; and, if the person has implicit faith, the whole being is governed by this one powerful direction of activity. Religiously speaking, the emotional experience unconsciously opens the soul to the Spirit, which enters into the whole being, just as the warm sunlight penetrates the very fibre of the plant. It is the Spirit that performs the mental part of the cure, not the personal thought or faith. The human part consists in becoming receptive, in withdrawing the consciousness from self and physical sensation, and becoming absorbed in the expected cure. The personal fears and wrong thoughts have stood in the way, and barred the door where the Spirit sought to enter. The new direction of mind changes all this, and makes way for the Spirit. It is a redirecting of the will; and in the wise use of the will, as we have seen, lies the greatest human power, while its misuse is the most potent cause of trouble.

Of all known forms of life, then, the energy that is set free by this changed attitude is the most important, the most powerful, and, probably, the least understood. Used ignorantly, it brings all our misery; used wisely, its power of developing health and happiness is limitless. It is essential to a just understanding of it, and to the knowledge of how to help one's self, that the reader bear in mind the central thought of each of the foregoing chapters. For we have learned that all power acts through something; and, in order to understand how the changed attitude may even affect bodily disease, one must remember how disease is built up.

To many people it seems impossible that a changed inner attitude can affect the bodily condition. Yet there are abundant illustrations of such change in emotional experiences such as those of religious conversion. As we have already seen, the mind is captivated, the new belief becomes a new rule for action. Moreover, the new attitude is accompanied by various subconscious and organic responses. The change is due to the alteration of the centre of equilibrium.* The response is not mental alone, but is also physical. The entire organism is stirred. The dormant life is quickened. All this results from a comparatively simple alteration in the life—so far as the active consciousness is concerned.

*See the account of religious conversion given by Professor James in "The Varieties of Religious Experience".

The point that here concerns us is not the subconscious or organic change, but the decisive state of mind, the new dynamic attitude. The results that ensue in various types of emotional experience may be brought about more gradually by intelligent application of the foregoing principles.

The first fact to note, then, is that the power of self-help is with us, like the air we breathe, ever awaiting our recognition. In the moments of calm decision before referred to, when we master our fears or decide upon this better conduct in preference to an unwise act, we do not have to fix the decision in mind, and say, "This shall be so." The decision itself is an act of will, like the desire to move the arm, and is put into effect unconsciously to us. In the same way the ideal of adjustment to life, and the daily effort to gain one's poise, is effective in proportion to the clearness and strength of our thought and the confidence we put into it. The first essential is a healthier and wiser habit of thought, for the ideas that we have inherited and grown up with narrow and cramp the inner life.

If the reader has carried out the suggestions of Chapter 1., and tried to actualise these vital truths in daily life, to realise the power of silent receptivity, it must already be clear that this is the most direct method of touching the inner centre. For, with the realisation of the presence of the immanent Spirit there comes the conviction that the Spirit is competent to minister to our truest and deepest need. A quieting influence, a sense of power and restfulness, falls upon the mind as a result of this realisation. The mere effort to become inwardly still is sufficient to awaken this sense of power, as though one were for the moment a magnetic centre toward which radiate streams of energy. And, if the reader has sought this silence in order to get relief from pain or some other uncomfortable sensation, there was doubtless a consciousness of pressure or activity in some part of the being, as though the resident power were trying to restore equilibrium. To unite in thought with this quickening power is, in general terms, the first step in the process of self-help by the silent method.

There is, obviously, no general rule which should govern the conscious process, because no two troubles and no two individuals are wholly alike. Sometimes one needs mental rousing; and the suggestion should be clear, strong, and decisive. Again, there should be little active thought; and, on general principles, the central thought of this volume—the power of silence—is at once the quickest and surest means of self-help. It is this power, and the attitude which invites it, which one should be conscious of—not of the pain, the fatigue, or the depression from which one wishes to be free. This power is shut out during trouble. There is resistance to it, and contraction in some part of the body. In order to overcome this resistance, one should "open out" inwardly, try to find the inward centre where the power is pressing through, or the centre of repose described in the foregoing chapter. Simply to search for it, and to rely upon this quickening power, is sufficient not only to draw the attention away from physical sensation, but to be immensely refreshed by the renewing presence. For, through this experience of receptivity—it is an experience rather than a process of thought—one becomes connected with a boundless reservoir of life and healing power. The healing process is, in fact, one form of receiving life. We do not originate life. We use it, we are animated by it; for it already exists. Our individual life is a sharing of universal life. We possess it by living it; and to partake of it is the commonest yet the highest privilege of man.

In order to make this experience vivid and clear, let us compare the soul to the budding life which is trying to open its petals and expand into a beautiful flower. The soul has been through a round of experiences in ignorance of their meaning. It has come into rude contact with the world, and has sought to withdraw from the world's wickedness and misery. In thus withdrawing, it has shut into a narrow space the mental pictures and remembrances of the experiences that were repulsive to it. It has narrowed and cramped itself into this prison of its own selfhood.

The tendency of the quiet, reposeful realisation of the divine presence is to touch the suppressed inner state and overcome the obstructions. The expanding process may not always be pleasant, and oftentimes one feels restless and impatient to have it completed. It may require long and trustfully persistent effort to overcome a condition of long standing. At times it is only necessary to open the inner being in silence for a few moments in order to take off the pressure and become wonderfully refreshed. Again, one finds it necessary to try all methods—read a comforting book, think of some friend, or a person in distress to whom one would like to be of service; rouse one's self with a firm determination to rise above this troublesome difficulty, or push through it with a persistently positive thought.

But in all cases one should approach this experience with a quiet confidence that the resident power is fully equal to the occasion. It is here with the imprisoned soul. Help abounds. The Spirit awaits our co-operation. We belong to it. We need not fear: we only need be open to it, to let it come, to let it have us and heal us. It knows our needs, and is never absent from us. We are not so badly off as we seemed, nor is there any reason for worry or discouragement. Peace, peace! Let us be still, quiet, restful, and calm. Let us know and feel the eternal Presence which is here to restore us, and to calm the troubled waters with its soothing love and peace.

In due time, if the realisation is repeated until one learns to be still and receptive, one will become conscious of benefit and a quickening of the whole being. The mere form of words is nothing, and the above expressions are simply used in the hope that they may suggest the indescribable; for, once more, it is the Spirit which is the essential, the power behind the words, the experience which all must have in order to know its depth and value.

The ability to concentrate is the secret of self-help by this method of realisation, and this is an art which each man learns in his own way. There must be a certain degree of self-possession, in order to hold the attention in a definite direction; and, if one have not yet developed this ability, it is well to approach this deeper realisation by degrees. The process of silent help is, in fact, one of adjustment to the actual situation in the moment of trouble—the realisation that, individually, one has little power, even of the will, as compared with this higher Will, but that all that is demanded of the individual will is co-operation. God seems to need us as much as we need Him. He asks thoughtful receptivity, and readiness to move with the deepest trend of the inner being. The experience is rather a wise directing of the will or attention, a realisation, an attitude, rather than a process of reasoning. The adjustment, the poise, the experience of silence, is a realisation. The moment comes when the individual has nothing to say: the conscious thought becomes subordinated to the sense of the divine Presence. One cannot speak. One can only observe in silent wonder, in awe at the presence of such power, which the individual feels incompetent to control. This is the highest aspect of the experience, the most effective, the least personal, yet the hardest to describe.* One can only say: Here is the Life, the Love, the Spirit. I have dwelt with it for a season. Go thou to the fountain-head, It will speak to you, and be its own evidence.

*Hence the reader must make allowances for the inadequate, figurative character of this account of the experience.

But sometimes one is unable to penetrate to the Source of all power and connect in thought with the Omnipresent Life. The Spirit seems far from one, and one feels wholly separate from it. In such cases it is better to make the realisation more personal, as one would rely on a friend who is ready to perform the slightest service and be a constant comfort during severe illness. One would naturally be drawn to such a friend in ties of close sympathy and trust. In moments of weakness and despair the friend would be one's better self, full of hope and cheer. It is in such times as this that our friends are nearest and dearest to us, that we open our souls to them and show what we really are. The mother's love, the friend's devotion, is thus the means of keeping many a person in this present life when all other means have failed—failed because they could not touch the soul,—whereas the communion of soul with soul through the truest affection opens the door to that higher Love which thus finds a willing object of its unfailing devotion.

Now, if in moments of trouble like these the reader will turn to the Spirit as to an intimate friend, help will surely come. The higher Power is still with one, but it is shut out. It is near, it is ready, like the friend, to help us, to guide, to strengthen, to advise, and to bestow comfort. One is momentarily disconnected from it and unaware of its promptings. One's personal self and activity stand in the way. The human will, fear, and all sorts of opinions have intruded, caused the Spirit to withdraw, and placed an obstacle in its pathway. To still the active personal self, to stand aside completely and let the Spirit return and fill the entire being, is, in a word, the secret of self-help in this as in all cases.

This is not easily done at first, and one is apt to force the wrong thoughts out of mind or try to reason them away. One often hears people say that they do not wish to think these wrong thoughts, but they cannot help it.

Suppose, for example, that one has a feeling of ill-will toward another, some unpleasant memory, or feels sensitive in regard to some word or act of a friend. Instead of trying to put away the unpleasant feeling by thinking about it, one should call the friend to mind and think of his or her good qualities, think of something pleasant, some good deed or some happy memory; for there is surely some good quality in every person. Very soon the unpleasant thought will disappear, and a sense of love and charity will take its place. It was not necessary to force it away, for one cannot hold both love and hatred at the same time.

In endeavouring to find the good side of the person who has said the unkind word or acted impulsively, one seems almost to enter into communion with the friend's soul, the real, the truest, and deepest person, who did not mean to act unkindly and who now regrets the unkindness. One's feeling of peace and forgiveness seems to reach the other soul. One is lifted above the petty, belittling self to the higher level of spiritual poise and restfulness. One has found one's own soul; and to find this, in moments of trouble, discouragement, sorrow, or sickness—this is self-help.

Here is the inner kingdom of heaven, where dwells all Love, Wisdom, and Peace, whence one may draw power at one's need and become readjusted to life. Here is where the permanent consciousness should abide. Here is the home of the greatest happiness and the truest health—a happiness and a health which only ask our recognition in order to become fully and consciously ours in daily life, morally, intellectually, and physically.*

*The author does not venture to assign limits to these optimistic methods of assisting nature, nor does he advise neglect of any of the common-sense methods of living. It remains for each reader to discover the practical value of the suggestions here given.

From the point of view of intellectual activity it is more difficult to find the inner centre and realise the power of silence. The intellect is apt to raise objections and to seek all the reasons for such a proceeding. But the experience must come first, then it may be rationalised. The empirical factor is of much more consequence than the theoretical explanation of it. If one permits the intellect to raise objections before the experience has become a matter of actual life, one may close the door entirely to the higher consciousness. The ordinary habits and thoughts of life are entirely foreign to any such experience. The generally accepted opinions and education prevent one from getting into this higher state. Its own knowledge, its pride of intellect and assurance, make it difficult for the mind to surrender; and there is consequently much more resistance to be overcome. One is apt to forget that, so far as one has come into possession of the truth, that truth is universal: it is not the property of the individual alone. The very intellect whereby the truth was discovered is a product or gift of the immanent Life, is an individualisation of the larger Intellect,—just as life is a sharing of the immanent and bountiful Life in which we dwell, and of which we are not in any sense independent. Only the mere opinion or belief is purely personal; and it is usually just this personal element that stands in the way; it is some harmful or borrowed opinion, which prevents one from getting real wisdom. It is humility, willingness to learn, which opens one to the Spirit; and, if one approaches this experience in a purely intellectual attitude, one is not likely to feel the' warmth of the Spirit.

In such cases, as, in fact, in all cases of trouble and suffering, the mind revolves in a channel that is too narrow. One needs to escape into a larger life, out of this narrow sphere of consciousness which has dwarfed and limited one's development. The very principles, and the habits, whereby one becomes devoted to a certain line of work to the exclusion of all others, cause the mind to act in given channels, and never to pass beyond them. If this process is long continued, with but little rest or recreation, nature is sure to rebel, and to warn us that we must be wiser and broader in our thinking. And probably the surest way of getting out of ruts, and thereby avoiding the long list of troubles which result from the constant pursuit of one idea, is to realise our relation to the universal Life in which our own qualities of intellect and power inhere, and which demands of us all-round development, that we may come into full self-possession and complete soul-freedom. Rightly used, then, the intellect is the basis, it gives the only firm basis on which to rest the superstructure of the spiritual life.

On the physical plane the first essential is to remember that the healing power is present in the body, ready to restore all hurts, and that, if one will keep still, like the animals, the result will be very different. On this plane one is in need of a wise counsellor to restore confidence and allay fear. The healing power meets with little or no resistance in the child; and, if medicine is kept away, and no disturbing influence or fear be allowed to interfere with the natural process, the mother can better fill this office than anyone else.

The best, the most lasting process of self-help, then, is the gradual acquirement of the wiser mode of life for which this whole volume pleads; for it is what we think and dwell upon habitually that is effective in the long run. Our inquiry has taught us to look beneath matter to its underlying Reality, and behind physical sensation to the mind by which it is perceived. We have found the origin of man, first, in the immanent Life of which he is a part, and of which he is an individual expression; and, secondly, in the world of mind, where his beliefs and impressions gather to form his superficial self. To know the one Self from the other, to be adjusted to its resistless tendency, to obey it, to do nothing contrary to it, as far as one knows, is the highest righteousness, the most useful life, and the truest religion. Here is the essential, the life that is most worthy of the man aware of his own origin and of his own duty.

It is everything to know that such possibilities exist, and to make a step toward their realisation. It is enough at first to be turned in the right direction; to feel that help is for us, and only awaits our receptivity; to have some inkling of the great Power of silence, All else will come in due course if one have a deep desire for it. And, if we have considered the essential, and begun to realise its deep meaning for ourselves and for our fellow-beings, the larger and more complex life of the outer world will be explained by the light and wisdom from within.

Chapter XIII
Entering the Silence

—

A GREAT deal has been said and written during the past few years about "entering the silence," as the phrase goes. Without doubt, most of the teaching under this head is of great value. We live in a nervous, hurrying age, and too much cannot be said about the resources of the meditative life. Nevertheless, certain vaguenesses have crept in, and some people have followed the wrong clue in their search for the values of silence. Recent tendencies have been so largely mystical that it is now necessary to differentiate more sharply than when the first edition of the present book was published. Moreover, certain problems have arisen that were not previously considered. It is important, then, to investigate the whole field afresh, not now for the purpose of suggestively describing the experience but for the sake of clearness.

1. The most superficial objection to the method that has been made is that, to "enter the silence" is to fall asleep. In such cases it may be that the experimenter needed rest, and if so nothing could have been better than sleep. Or, it may be that there was too much relaxation, a mere "letting go" rather than a change of activity. But mere relaxation is only a beginning. The essential is uplifting, enriching meditation, and meditation is not mere quietude. It is doubtful if a purely passive mental state is a possibility for any individual, under any circumstances. Hence, to surrender all activity is to lose consciousness in sleep. On the other hand, to meditate successfully is to combine wise, discriminative receptivity with uplifting activity. It is not then a question of eliminating activity, but of substituting reposeful for nervous activity. It is the nervous wear and tear that works mischief. To stop this is to be ready once more to return to work. Usually this nervous activity is restricted to a very limited region. To conquer the nervousness one must approach it with "the power of silence." The emphasis is upon the "power" rather than upon the "silence."

2. A faithful devotee of the doctrine once triumphantly exclaimed that now, at last, she could "enter the silence," for she could make her mind a "perfect blank." Now, it is often desirable to fall into a revery, with no definite thought in mind. But to make the mind a "blank" would be to fall asleep. During the waking hours the stream of consciousness constantly flows, and it is a question what trains of thought to give attention to, what ones to disregard or inhibit; for one must always give attention to something. One cannot empty the mind. But one may fill it with a chosen series of thoughts. To withdraw the attention from particular

objects would be to scatter one's powers and cultivate mere vagueness. This is precisely the course one should not pursue. For it is development that is desired, not reversion to the great "undifferentiated." To the cultivation of this habit of vagueness is due nearly all that is undesirable in spiritual meditation.

3. The notion that the mind should be made a "blank" is closely connected with another misunderstanding, namely, in regard to concentration. In the first place, it has been erroneously supposed that the mind can concentrate with no definite object to dwell upon; and in the second place, it has been though that concentration is a sustained act of voluntary attention. These suppositions are psychologically as ungrounded as the notion that there can be a mental state of pure passivity.

It is a very common error to conclude that if the attention shifts one lacks the power of concentration. But careful observation confirms the statement made by Professor James, that "there is no such thing as voluntary attention sustained for more than a few seconds at a time. What is called sustained voluntary attention is a repetition of successive efforts which bring back the topic to mind. The topic once brought back, if a congenial one, develops . . . . no one can possibly attend continuously to an object that does not change."

Successful concentration consists, then, in continuous acts of attention given to various details of the object under consideration. No one can long attend to one idea. In fact an idea lingers but a moment. The succeeding moment brings, at best, only an idea that resembles it. It is not only impossible to hold the attention in one direction, without a break, but it is undesirable to try to do this. No one should be discouraged who finds that the attention shifts from phase to phase of the general trend of consciousness. This is the way of nature. Consciousness lives; it is not a dead affair. In all life there is change. The attainments which eventually come out of the realm of change are due to a succession of little movements. Unity is won by moving in a general direction. And likewise with the mind, unity or concentration is attained by continually bringing the attention back to the point. One should give no thought to the wanderings of attention, but simply turn the mind once more in the chosen direction.

To concentrate, then, is to gather the scattering lines of consciousness and focus them upon a unifying idea. Concentration is a highly active mental state, not mere passivity, or "letting go." To concentrate is to exclude. If your "silence" is to be of an uplifting sort, you must wisely select a line of profitable thinking, then give your mind so fully to it that undesirable thoughts will be shut out. If the consciousness of sensation intrudes, never mind the intrusion; fill your mind more actively with the thought which you wish to meditate upon. To be restfully silent is of course to be calm within. But it is a choice between activities, not between activity and passivity. If you are to meditate in peace you must be peaceful. But to be peaceful you must be so strong in your attitude of inner poise that no other activity can break into your concentrated repose. "Power through repose" is Miss Call's phrase, that is, the power of repose, not the weakness of it. The majority of people are rather loosely put together. What they need is not to dangle and "let go," but to take hold of themselves and turn their reorganised life into a wise channel.

Again, some devotees of the "silence" have thought that there was some sort of mysterious power or feeling which one might enter into by opening the mind in what they called a "spiritual" direction. Hence they have entered the silence with no particular idea in mind. Now, it is desirable to help people out of the thought of "mysteries," not into them. It is the clear-cut, the intelligible idea, that is the desirable. To set out upon a vague search for the mysterious is to open the door to all sorts of abnormal mental experiences. It is because of this that so many have found it altogether imprudent to try to enter the silence at all. But the trouble lay in themselves. We find what we look for. If you believe in the occult, you will invite it. If you are in search of the sane, the quicker you cut loose from all vague groping after the mysterious the better.

For the majority, then, it is far wiser to choose an entirely definite idea, such as a passage from Scripture, and make the silent hour a decidedly intelligent religious experience, with clear-cut ideals in view. For it is fineness of thinking, the kind of thinking which refines, uplifts, purifies, that brings about the desirable states of repose. Such thinking clarifies the brain, whereas the vacuity above referred to muddles it. Some people in these days have given themselves over to this vagueness to such an extent that they seem to have lost the power of discrimination. But unless one can discriminate one had better not try to enter the silence. If, then, you are unable to discover a refining thought of your own which will make your meditation definite, it would be well for you to read some uplifting book until you find an idea that is worth thinking about.

Do not then begin your meditation with a revery. After you have actually settled down into restfulness, and found a desirable idea to dwell upon, that is, after you have thought for a while, you may well yield yourself to the mood you find yourself in. But it is the active linking which leads to this, and what goes on in a state of revery is subconscious "brooding" over some absorbing idea. Hence it is that a revery is oftentimes very productive. Granted an interesting thought, the mind is able to develop it. But if you put no corn in your mill you will have no meal; if you put in poor material you will produce poor results.

It is plain that we are considering the same thing under two heads. To concentrate is to discriminate, and one cannot discriminate unless one gives selective attention. The trouble, then, has been vagueness in regard to what the whole process of "entering the silence" is for. The feeling side of life has been cultivated at the expense of the intellectual. But to know what it is well to feel, that is, what sentiments are worthy of increase, one must first use one's wits. Mere indiscriminate "letting go" is never desirable. But to go apart from "the madding crowd" and think for one's self in wise solitude is highly desirable. Moreover, it is well to know how to absent one's self from any environment one may chance to be in. To possess this power one must know how to concentrate. Concentration, then, is the beginning; and this is far simpler, after all, than many have thought. The essential is first to have a clear idea of what concentration is not, then busy one's self with what it is, that is, the persistent doing of whatever line of activity is chosen. We are concentrating all the time, while we go about our daily tasks. There is nothing mysterious about it. Why not "enter the silence," then, in the same common-sense sort of way that you would set about to make bread or kindle a fire? You can make a fine art of housework as well as of anything else. And there is more that is sound and wise in the well-ordered home than in all the occult gatherings that were ever gathered to meditate upon the indiscriminate.

4. Again, we see the vast importance not only of a sound theory of first principles but of intellectual standards, definite conclusions in regard to what is worthwhile. Vagueness concerning spiritual meditation springs largely out of the tendency to revert to Oriental pantheism and the Yogi practices. To accept mysticism in theory is to accept it in practice. To reject it philosophically is to reject it in conduct. Hence the vast importance of Christian theism in contrast with all pantheistic systems.

The crucial question is this: Is God known through sense? If we conclude that He is, we at once put Him on the same level with ourselves. To lower Him to the sense-level is to reject all the distinctions which make intelligible our thought of Him as the Father. When all relationships have been reduced to a dead level, the door is opened wide to all the illusions and errors of mysticism. It is then easy to say, "I and God are one," to put the emphasis on the "I," and hence to arrive at the point where all mysticism arrives—unless it is exceedingly careful—namely, at the stage of mere egoism, if not egotism. It is but one step more to announce that " all is good," hence to sweep away all ethical distinctions.

Christian theism very carefully distinguishes between God, the Father, and man, the worshipper. The Father is always in some sense above the personal self, or He is not known as the Father. To reduce Him to the realm of feeling is to mistake physical sensation for religious ecstasy, An untold number of illusions follow.

Only in the attitude of sonship does one maintain the right consciousness of relationship. The fact of Father-son relationship implies many considerations which lead directly away from pantheism.

One may of course hold that the divine presence is far more directly made known in the intimate precincts of the soul than through objective experience. But the closest relationship is still a relation, not an identification. Whatever the facts of the highest religious experience, it is clear that the experience means much or little according to the values attributed to it. Each man's account of it betrays his grade of development. As a matter of fact and as an affair of values, the experience is plainly relative. Hence the description of it should differentiate its various factors.

5. The fundamental error on the part of those who confuse the religious experience is undoubtedly the misconception of the place and value of the intellect. Throughout religious history one finds that the mystically inclined are either intellectually deficient, or have arrived at the conclusion that truth cannot be known through the intellect. This of course means that the revelation of God's presence is theoretically limited to the realm of feeling. No conclusion could be more inconsistent. For no one puts more emphasis upon the (intellectual) inferences drawn from the facts of religious experience than the devotee of mere feeling or mystic intuition. The chief difference between the rationalist and the mystic is that the former pursues his inferences to the end while the latter is satisfied with imperfect and unscrutinised conclusions.

Now, it requires but little reflection to discover that feeling comes first; immediate experience relates the mind to something objective, then thought seeks the meaning of that experience. The devotee of mere feeling in the religious world corresponds to the sensationalist in the world of nature. It is the province of the idealist to correct the inferences of both, and point out that only by rational scrutiny may one learn what is real. The idealist is as ready as anyone to recognise the primacy of given experience, but he points out that, for better or worse, experience has the reality and meaning which ideas sign to it. Hence the importance of a fundamental inquiry into the nature of experience.

It is precisely by virtue of the searching analyses of reason that one is able at last to discriminate the sound from the unsound in the realm of feeling, to avoid the pitfalls of pantheism, yet preserve the values which are rightly attributable to the higher religious experiences. It may even be said that God is knowable only through reason, for not until one rationally tests the pronouncements of experience is one able to differentiate sensation from the finer sentiments, to distinguish the human will from the divine love. Nothing is of greater importance, then, in the inner life than a sound idea of God. For the idea is the clue to wise adjustment, the principle of right action. The clearer and more carefully considered the idea, the saner will be the conduct that is shaped by it. There could be no greater mistake, then, than to suppose it to be wrong to try to understand the soul's relationship to God.

The relative worth of the intellect once understood, one is in a position to pursue the empirical inquiry to the end, to discover the values of the meditative life, and enjoy the benefits of silence. For each new experience becomes food for thought, and hence is of value for conduct. In the long run one learns that it is not mere accumulation of feelings that gives power and worth to life. Simply to pass through an experience is only to enter the first stage of development. It is the thought and the conduct that follow which test the experience. Hence the importance of mere receptivity should not be exaggerated.

In the long run, also, it is systematic intellectual development that most directly helps the mind to concentrate. For it is the intellect that organises, defines. The intellect contributes the form, the method, makes clear the principle or law. Granted the organisation, one is free to fill it with the spirit. Hence it is balance between spirit and form that is desirable.

The foundation of composure is philosophical conviction. It is not faith without reason, but faith rationally scrutinised and developed that gives this conviction. Hence we have seen the importance throughout our inquiry of keen discrimination and the gradual development of a theory of life. As valuable as first-hand experience may be, it is rendered far more valuable by reflection. Moreover, we have seen the importance of discernment between the lower and higher levels of consciousness. It is the reduction to a dead level, the confusion between higher and lower that is responsible for many of the false inferences of the religious devotee. The experiences on the heights are no doubt of great value, but reason is alone capable of discerning their sanity. The higher carefully distinguished from the lower, one is free to develop the resulting data into a system. The more highly developed the system, the profounder is one's basis of repose. And after awhile one no longer cares for aught that is mystical. Experience proves that it is far more profitable to turn to the works of the really great philosophers for inspiration than to the works of rambling essayists.

6. Another objection to the method of " entering the silence" is that it is an artificial device made necessary, it may be, by the needs of our nervous, hurrying age. Ordinarily, it is said, one should avoid introspection.

This criticism is sound in large part. The "silence" is a device, of temporary value, easily leading into one-sided individualism, to the neglect of urgent social problems. If men always maintained a sanctuary of the spirit in the inner life, it would not be necessary to seek "the silence" self-consciously. It is inner silence as a habit that is desirable. It is only necessary to give specific attention to the process in so far as the objective life intrudes upon the solitudes within. And introspection is only a passing stage in the experience. The ideal is to penetrate beyond mere self-consciousness to the holy of holies, to uplift the soul in worship, breathe a silent prayer to the Father.

Yet from another point of view the criticism is unfair, since it is a law of the spiritual life that renewed consecration is the beginning of all fresh activity; and the silent communion at its best is consecration. Regarded in this way, the experience is thoroughly normal, sound and sane. It is not the device of the sickly, or the resource of the nervously inclined; but is a glad moment of recreation on the part of the man who worships God "in spirit and in truth." It is a rediscovery of the primal sources of the spiritual life on the part of those who no longer find values in external symbols. It is the natural act of the self-reliant soul, an expression of the freedom of true individuality; and hence valuable as a means to an end.

7. Let us then endeavour to restate some of the values of the experience as concretely as possible. In the first place, there is need of readjustment. Life has become for the moment too complex, one is trying to accomplish over-much in a given hour or day. Hence there is great waste of energy and withal increasing nervous tension. The resource is to take the text "Sufficient for each day is its own trouble." *

*This is the literal rendering of Matthew, vi., 34.

It is a revelation to many people who have sought to enter fully into the present to discover how largely their consciousness is ordinarily concerned with distant things. The attention is constantly turned here and there by thoughts that disturb one's repose. The past is regarded with regret, the future with fear and suspicion. Neglected duties occur to consciousness, and there is a sense of uncertainty in regard to what the mind ought to be engaged in. The thought occurs that perhaps one ought to be elsewhere, instead of taking time for a quiet meditation. One has set aside precisely half an hour for thought and one watches the clock lest one overstep the limit. The nervous, hurrying tide of our modern life pulses through all one's thinking, and not for one moment is the mind in repose.

Consequently, if you really wish to profit by a half-hour's meditation make up your mind to put aside everything else. If duties occur to mind, decide when you will attend to them, and immediately dismiss them. When the past comes up laden with regret, leave it to bury its own dead. Tell the future that you will attend to it when it arrives. If part of your consciousness is flying north, part south and the rest up and down, call it in from all directions, as if you were drawing in an arm, gathering your forces unto yourself. Settle down reposefully upon your chair. Let the present little environment contain all there is of you. When the mind flies off again, bring it back. Yield yourself to the moment in full enjoyment. Disconnect from the rushing currents of modern thought, and become as moderate as if you were back in the old stage-coach days, before the era of record-breaking express trains and automobiles. Do not simply banish all thoughts from your mind, but whatever you think let your thoughts radiate, as it were, from the eternal present. Remember that you are a soul dwelling in eternity. Live in the thought of eternity for a while, and let the world of time rage on.

If you do not see what is wise for you to do next year, what plans you ought to adopt for the coming month, what you should do tomorrow, ask yourself if there is something for you to do today. The chances are that you will find something that is very well worth doing today. Probably you will find more in the living present than you can attend to, and there you were borrowing trouble for next year! When you have settled upon the wisest thing for today, do it as well as you can. Put your whole soul into it, let it be an artistic, philosophical performance. When that is well done you will readily see what to do next.

This resource never fails. When in doubt about the future, when in need of guidance, we can, at least, be true to the best we know now. That is all that anyone can ask of us. It is not necessary to consult a book or seek out a prophet. Within the breast there is a guide for all. The wise tendency of the present is related to the wisdom of all time. Brush all else aside, discover that tendency and move forward with it, and the way into the future will open.

This is a perfectly familiar thought—that the problem of today is sufficient unto today. Yet it is no small attainment to learn how to live in the present. It is a good rule to follow throughout the day, not simply during one's half-hour of silent seclusion. The silent time is needed largely as a preparation for the remainder of the day. Put yourself into the present, make a fresh start, then make a determined effort to stand by the present. If you catch yourself scattering your forces, living past, present and future all at once, call yourself back into the living today. Draw in your mental arms, gather your powers into yourself, and once more start out. It is really a source of genuine pleasure—this full participation in the activity of life while it is yet here, as it passes. Not until we live reposefully do we begin to experience the benefit of our powers. Each of us has a certain amount of power. That power is sufficient to carry us through life in health, strength and happiness, with abundant liberty to do good and profit by experience. Our powers may, of course, be increased. But right here and now we have sufficient power to live sanely if we would but possess it, acquire poise and use our Power wisely. The waste of energy in the average human machine is enormous.

We waste energy by the way we walk, by nervous habits of eating, talking, working, and the like. There is an economical, rhythmical way to spend our forces which will spare us the nervous wear and tear. It is the little interior tension and excitement which is most wearing. One need not become a slow-coach in order to avoid this nervous waste of force. It is possible to move rapidly yet harmoniously, reposefully. Possess yourself within, be at home in your own mental world, and you may move as quickly as you please on the surface.

Some people wonder how it is that others who do not seem to be physically strong are able to do so much more in the same length of time. Here is one of the secrets. They have learned how to work. They do one thing at a time, and they do that well, moderately. They live for the time being in and for that particular activity, and there is no wear and tear due to borrowing trouble from other things.

Put in other terms, the attitude of which I am speaking is optimistic. It is a state in which one is willing to trust that the future will bring what is wise and right. Pessimism scatters force and borrows trouble galore. Optimism conserves our energies and does not even anticipate plans. Pessimism kicks against the pricks and creates friction. Optimism moves with the harmonious tide of life, and is content to be carried forward. All these states are within our control. All of us may learn to live in the present. If the present is full of hardship, the best way to overcome the hardship is to meet it here and now. Our trials do not seem so hard when we settle down to meet them in their own environment. For the same circumstances which bring the trial also bring the power to meet it. All that we need is here. There is no need to complain of the universe. But we must do our part by learning how to live wisely and profoundly in the eternal present.

Finally, life in the present opens the way to the discovery of untold resources in the mental world. For not until we begin the experiment do we learn the richness of our present thoughts. There is much wisdom awaiting recognition. Ordinarily we are too active to discover it. When we begin to settle down reposefully we learn that the soul is a centre of revelation, an organ of the divine life; that each individual point of view is of worth in relation to ultimate truth. Much wisdom will be made known through us when we become silent enough and receptive enough to perceive it. To live in the present is truly to become ourselves, and to become one's self is to serve the higher Power. We know not who and what we are until we thus begin to live. Thus to live is to discover that we are also members of an eternal order of being where time matters not at all.

Chapter XIV
The Outlook

—

LET us now look back over the field of our investigation and note the general results, that we may know what sort of philosophy is implied in the discussions as a whole. We were first concerned with the method of inquiry which we found must be threefold. (1) There is the realm of fact, of life as we find it, with all its wealth of experiences and its problems. We awaken into existence to find ourselves played upon and moving forward amidst a stream of circumstances, more or less plastic. The desire arises to understand the laws and conditions of this multi-form existence, so that we may live more wisely, and be of greater service to our fellows. We find the clue to this wiser mode of thinking and living in the very problems that suggest philosophical endeavour. (2) But in order to carry forward the philosophical investigation successfully it is necessary for us to distinguish between life as it is presented, on the one hand, and life as we take it, on the other. Besides the facts, there are the values which we assign to them, the ideals we strive for, the theories we propose. Evidently we must discriminate closely, in order to discover our actual situation in life. (3) Finally, there is the mode of Life which expresses our beliefs and ideals. To enter into fuller possession of the genuine reality of things, we must more truly acquaint ourselves with life at first hand. The test of our philosophy is found in conduct. We must therefore brush away artificialities and experiment afresh. When we attain a truer adjustment we shall be able to improve our theories.

We then turned to a consideration of the divine immanence. The discussion was a bit abstruse for a time, but in due course we saw the deeper significance of this reasoning. It was the empirical factor, the higher consciousness of man, that proved to be of prime importance. The essential was the import of the divine life in all its immanent forms. Hence we saw the importance of adapting life with a view to the fuller realisation of the spiritual ideal. The purpose of life proved to be largely dependent on the meaning we derive from it, according to our interpretation of the universe. Yet we saw the importance of distinguishing between the world of our mental life, and the tangibly real world of nature, with its laws and evolutions.

Having acknowledged the realities of the objective world, we were next concerned with the world of our own consciousness. We found that it was largely a question of overcoming the illusions which beset ordinary experience. For we have always been conscious beings, the world has always been made known through mind.

Once in possession of the idealistic clue, we are able to correct the illusions of materialistic theories, to become at home in the mental world, and look about in a spirit of leisure.

The first discovery led to many others, and we found that life is not only fundamentally mental, but is also social and active. From this point on it was a question of tracing the connections between the dynamic attitudes of the soul and the various moods, beliefs, and notions which influence conduct. From one point of view, life appeared to be what our thinking makes it. We found a surprising amount of evidence for this supposition. But closer analysis revealed the fact that many of our mental states are purely ephemeral and superficial. Therefore we concluded that only the thoughts that win our attention and become objects of action are of much consequence in actual experience. What we really believe is shown by what we do. From the facts of conduct we may retrospectively discover what beliefs and mental attitudes are really instrumental.

We also found it necessary to distinguish between the world as it is continuously presented to us from without, and the world of our own wills. When evidence is brought forward that we live a mental life, the inference sometimes is that human consciousness shapes life, hence one may make the world what one wills. We found evidence, indeed, that whatever one believes is gospel truth for the time being—for the one who believes it. But that does not make it true in the divine order. In fact, our belief may be so far from the truth that we may be living in a dream world of our own fancy. Thus the origin is seen of the self-centering egoisms into which the mere thought theory develops.

As matter of fact, so we concluded, it does not give man one whit more license to discover that he lives a life of mind. He simply discovers that, instead of being a physical body, he is a conscious soul. Many additional conclusions follow which lead to the emphasis of the soul rather than the body. Law still reigns. Matter must still be distinguished from mind, and man must adapt himself to the conditions of natural existence. He still has social obligations. The divine tendency is still with him. The discovery points to the within and the beyond. But man is as dependent as ever. His responsibilities have increased. His opportunities have multiplied many times. It is not until we pass beyond the domain of the merely human that the situation is much changed. Then we possess a foundation for the unity of life which renders all else secondary.

The great fact in all the universe about us and especially in the world of the soul, is the existence of the Spirit, ever in manifestation, possessing what we in our feeble speech call a "constitution," an "organism." That is, God is orderly. Since He is one, and His life is a system, fraught with purpose, inspired by centralising love, all His universe is orderly. The world over, God's life moves in uniformity, is exemplified by what we call law. His will, His oneness of purpose is thus the true basis of unity. Whether in the inner life or the outer, God is the same. The distinctions of nature, man and man, mind and matter, are not separations of God from God.

Conscious of himself, within this great system, exists man, environed by activities of that Life, expressed in various forms. Some forms are conveniently distinguishable as belonging to nature, some to mind, and some to the moral domain. But all is from one great Life, and the question is, What is the dynamic relation of the soul to the activities of that Life, the laws which it reveals, and the ideal tendencies which it manifests? It matters not what the order of being, the question is the same. Thus the problem of life is a spiritual problem. There is an ideal for each, a tendency resident in each. How far is the soul aware of and in adjustment with that tendency, how far does it choose that ideal, instead of its own will? There may be ways of temporary escape, methods of glossing over that which is ugly. But in the end the soul must come face to face with itself and ask the test question.

As all laws and forces centre about the divine Being at large, so we may say that the universe for the individual centres about the soul. Our conclusion that life is primarily conscious points to that centre, for all that we know of the world in the last analysis is reducible to the ideas and activities immediately related to and known by the soul. It is a large world that surrounds the soul—the universe of nature, man and God; it is a relatively small world where man, the observer, watches the world-play in relation to his mental states. Formerly he believed himself to be an objective being of flesh and blood; now he finds that behind the most intimately subjective mental states he, the real individual, lives. In so far as he plays a part in the great world around him, here is the decisive centre where all choices are made, where all action begins. Sometimes it seems that the turning of a feather would suffice to settle between alternatives.

Formerly, we complained of the universe because of the pains we suffered; we cast the blame on people, things, on God, anyone, anything but on self. We were in a continual attitude of fault-finding, dislike and fear. We were practically materialists. We regarded causation, influence, power as arising from outside. Therefore we led a kind of life which this materialistic conclusion implies. Or rather it was not a conclusion; it was a thoughtless taking of the world of things without thinking about it. But when philosophical thought began, that incomparably valuable discovery that what life yields us is largely conditioned by what we bring to it, the whole face of things was changed. It is not, as we have already noted, that our human thought actually changes the world, but that it changes the world for us. When the awakening comes we realise that nothing under God's fair sky can change life from the old way to the new except our own change of thought, action, and attitude. We must "reform it altogether," as Shakespeare says. It does not suffice to think other thoughts; we must do other deeds, adopt a different dynamic attitude towards the whole of life.

In the first place, all blame should cease, for it was not things that enslaved us, but ideas; not other people, but ourselves; not God, but our own condition of development. Other people are as ignorant as we were, therefore we will not blame them. We knew not that our attitude was wrong, therefore we will spend no time in regret, but "about face" and begin anew. The tender love of the Father was ever-present, though misunderstood and opposed, therefore we could have asked nothing more of God. The entire organism of life is ready, at our service, guidance is here, law, order. Everything, then, depends on the degree of our earnestness. We awake to knowledge of the fact that we are reaping as we have sowed and that we may sow and reap anew. It matters little what the particular experience was. It may have been a lost opportunity on our part, indolence, impulsiveness, imprudence in the use of money, improvidence, unkind criticism by which we excluded ourselves from society, hatred, aristocracy, or something of that kind. It may have been narrowness, meanness, too close calculation, or selfishness in some of its many forms. Whatever the mental state, it really amounted to thoughtlessness, which in turn was due to lack of self-control. The way of escape is therefore plain; there must be more consciousness at the centre, more poise and moderation. We can depend on the universe to give back action for action. What could be plainer, more mathematical, more satisfactory than this? We are reaping as we have sown. We sow from within. We can sow more wisely. We shall reap hereafter as we sow now.

Was it a "mistake" that we made? Yes, relatively speaking. In the end, no; for it is only thus that we learn. It is only through suffering that we learn the greatest lesson of life. Everyone who has suffered deeply and seen the meaning of suffering acknowledges that. Suffering compels us to think, and in course of time we come to judgment. The price is not high in the light of the rich compensation. Only so far as we overcome do we acquire greater power. It is suffering, too, which brings the greatest revelation of our dependence on the Father. It is suffering which reveals the true self, which shows the real significance of life. Life is primarily for the soul—so these deeper revelations teach us. We are immortal beings, sons of God. This comparatively low round of the ladder on which we awaken to find ourselves is but the beginning of real life. We graduate from level to level in so far as we meet our opportunities and manifest the soul. And the soul—what is that? Not the merely human ego which comes to consciousness of its powers and learns to sow anew; but an heir of the love of God, whose privilege it is to serve in the spiritual kingdom, to advance into a realm so much larger that all previous life will seem insignificant in comparison.

The philosophical principle which helps the mind to see the unity of the spiritual with the mental and physical states is the law of contrast, or evolution from lower to higher. While man is still unaware of the meaning of this duality he condemns himself for possessing a lower nature. His error is in endeavouring to understand the lower by itself. This is the error of physical science from first to last. In truth, any given thing is only to be understood by reference to the purpose, end, motive, the ideal which is to be realised through it. The egg is to become, or may become, the fowl. By itself it is more or less of a mystery. Man is in truth a spiritual being, and the true significance of his struggles is only to be understood in the light of the fulness of soul-life which is to come out of them. This is the profoundest truth of evolution, it is the solution of the problem of evil. For evil is the manifestation of the lower when there is a higher, the pursuit of inferior methods when there is a superior way. In man the human is added to the animal. That which would have been right for the animal becomes the passion which tests man in his spiritual growth. It is through the contests of lower and higher that man finally comes to consciousness. The clue to the whole is the discovery that contrast, conflict, is essential to evolution, at least up to a certain point; and that in so far as man is conscious of his forces he may transmute the same energy which would have been spent on the lower plane into the higher life.

Suppose, for example, that someone approaches me in anger, and with show of violence. The natural tendency of the animal in me is to give back violence for violence. But if I pause for a moment to consider I disconnect my wire, as it were, from the lower motor and attach it to a higher. I adopt an attitude of forgiving peace, I make only a gentle reply; and thus lift the spirit of the whole occasion. Here, in a word, is the whole process of transmutation. When we see the meaning of it all, the whole aspect of life is changed. It is no longer good and evil at war, but lower and higher, both essential to evolution, and both furthering our progress in so far as we rightly understand and wisely adjust. Here is the unity of life once more.

In truth, then, as we saw in Chapter IX., there are two types of consciousness. When we understand these we have the key to the situation. On the lower level the mind is more or less conditioned by the body. The mind feels certain pains, tendencies, moods, and temptations, and thinks these are of the truer self. On the higher level these conditions are transcended, the mind knows that these are lower than the truer self, and therefore it does not judge by them. (1) Here is an astrological prophecy, for example, foreboding ill, and perfectly true on its own plane. (2) But here are higher powers which are as superior to the stream on the lower level as love is superior to hate. (1) Here is consciousness absorbed in pain, and (2) here is consciousness dwelling, not on the process, but on the outcome. (1) Here is a mood which inspires doubt, fear, despondency; and (2) here is another which looks through it to the sunlight beyond. Once understand this relationship, learn how your moods are conditioned, and it is only a question of time when you will be able to live continuously in the superior realm, whatever comes. Then that which would once have been a temptation will be an opportunity for strength. A fear is an idle zephyr. A doubt is a ripple on the surface. An annoyance is a source of amusement. A curse is a blessing. A selfish sentiment is known as such and permitted to slay itself. Each and every time the soul takes its clue from the ideal, calmly settles down in trust, isolates the consciousness from the lower, thus drawing away its power; and lets "things work." The secret is, live on the higher plane, push through, out and above, glide over, hold to the ideal, see the end, transcend the means, trust, wait, rest, "dare all nor be afraid.". "And I, if I be lifted up from the earth, will draw all men unto me."

Thus there is a twofold clue to the wise attitude towards life. On the one hand, there is right philosophical thinking about the universe, in terms of law, order, unity, evolution, and consciousness. On the other hand, there is the spiritual realisation of what the life, the power, is, who we are and what we are here for. There is first right understanding, then right adjustment. The course of life is traced to the inner world, the power of individual thought and action. Then the personal life-stream is traced out into the universal where no man liveth unto himself. The philosophically spiritual life, then, is one wherein every moment is lived with more or less vivid consciousness of what we are all existing in. It is inspired by the concrete sense of the divine presence, the holiness of things. It ever has in remembrance the fact that we are dwellers in eternity, that whatever we are or may be called externally we are souls within, sons of God. Here is the standard by which to judge all questions, settle all difficulties. We should ask, Is this worthy of a son of God? Am I adjusting all things with reference to the highest standard I know? If so, then all things may be permitted to fall into line; we may let things drop into a secondary place, while ideas, deeds, occupy the first. There will be a gradual inner advance, a refinement; and a consequent transcending of minor objects of interest—the old man will die for want of attention while the new grows stronger day by day.

What sort of ideal should one keep before the mind? The ideal of constant advancement, of ever-widening circles, while enjoying the benefits of all our natural and social relations. The spirit is first, the inner life, the gifts of wisdom and love are at one's disposal. Here one sees more in a flash than can be carried out in years. Then there is the manifestation through form, the slower carrying out through the intellect; and the yet slower response of the physical organism. It is important to remember that we move at these three different paces—the quick-acting spirit, the moderate, opposing intellect, and the sluggish body. The soul must have patience while the new vision is being taken into the understanding. It should be yet more lenient with the slowly regenerating body. We need times to "catch up with ourselves," as someone has said. Many of our difficulties arise from neglect of this evolutionary, leavening process. This fact and the fact of our lower and higher consciousness are two of the most important facts of the spiritual life.

Thus the most persistent characteristic of our discussion is the many-sidedness of man, or, in other words, the fact that we must look at all things from a two-fold or relational point of view. There is a polarity or duality running through things which in the end is the surest clue to unity. Our life begins in consciousness, yet consciousness is nothing without relation to man, to nature, and God. The infant discovers the world and other selves, then itself, by contrast and relation. Our entire knowledge is developed by comparison of relations, by contrast. By contrast everything is distinguished. Thus we put darkness against its opposite, light. We separate worthy from unworthy actions, truth from error, selfishness from love. We are constantly turning from opposite to opposite. Life is a series of opposites, actions and reactions, inner and outer, up and down, male and female, centripetal and centrifugal. If we regard this duality as a warfare, life is a mystery for us. If we see the dependence of opposites, life is for us a living unity. One member of the duality could no more be taken from man's inner life than the centrifugal or the centripetal force could be withdrawn from the solar system. It is essential to human existence and evolution that lower and higher exist together. Man vibrates between the two and thus little by little discovers the meaning of his contrasted experiences.

The great discovery is the one already referred to, namely, that the only way to understand the lower is by reference to the higher. Nature is incomprehensible alone; it must be seen in relation to God whom it manifests. Man's body is unintelligible without the soul. The soul cannot be known without the Over-soul. The strife usually called "evil" is not then a warfare of good and evil forces; for that which tries to pull us down is as necessary as that which is eager to lift us up. We entirely misunderstand if we condemn the one as good and the other as evil. Either force carried to excess brings pain. Virtue becomes vice if carried too far. Vice also becomes virtue by reaction from excess. The friction resides in neither force alone; it is the lack of adjustment between them. The real meaning of our long vibration between extremes is our search for harmony. If we could attain such adjustment as the harmony which the revolutions of the planets exemplify we should scarcely know that there are two forces. Harmony is the perfect balance of opposites; it cannot exist without the two.

Let us then understand this duality through and through, as a law of life. Let us seek first that calmness which spares us the petty frictions of life, then gradually attain adjustment. Since it is the little interior friction, the mental worry and the nervous tension which wears us out, we should pause and let down the tension, take off the strain. Inner poise we must have if we would be outwardly at peace; and poise is a balance of opposites, a nice adjustment such that we move along with the stream of life, instead of against it. We are neither impatient nor indolent. We are not trying to manage the universe. We are not pushing society. Nor are we urging our own life forward in a wilful way. We are taking the pace at which the universe is going, content to let God take His own time. We desire above all that His will, not ours, shall be done. Thus we move out from the deep centre of consciousness to measured deeds of expression, service, love. This is not only the secret of health but the secret of wise life as a whole. All the friction is worthwhile which leads the way to this splendid result.

The whole of life is an adjustment to forces which play upon us from outside and the resistance which they meet within. Our inner life is not only a duality of lower and higher, but each inner contrast corresponds to an outer condition. We are like spheres whose surfaces present varying combinations. We start out in life, ignorant of our many-sidedness. Now we brush against this person, now against that one. Friction results where we dislike, harmony where we like. We are inclined to choose only the pleasant, but in due time we learn that the greatest growth sometimes comes from the mastery of dislikes and frictions. Even when we draw closer to those we love there is friction, till we learn to bear and forbear. If on one side of my social sphere I am too easily influenced, I may by taking thought overcome my weakness and grow strong. If on another side I use pressure, I must substitute love. Thus I continue to clash or to harmonise, until on all sides I have touched the world. Each time the clue to harmony is this duality of inner and outer. The soul is not independent, not adequate by itself. It must have an environment. The environment calls out the soul, and the soul contributes to the environment. Neither one is intelligible without the other.

The essential is a calm, philosophical view of the situation, so that as we brush against people and things we will know what this contact means, know that first of all the result of the relation will depend upon ourselves, but that the personal self is not all. In all relations we must take the two factors into account, the inner and the outer. For nothing stands by itself, "nothing is fair or good alone." The goodness of things, their beauty is found in relation. Life does not exist for one end alone but for many, in organic harmony. Life is a discipline of the understanding, as well as a training ground for the will; a world of the heart and a world of the head. It is for beauty, truth, expression, society, and many other ends; and to attain all these one must have manifold interests, and subdivide one's time. The ideal is the perfect whole, balance, proportion. We must therefore round out our being, and feel in harmony with, apprehend the larger whole of the universe. This is the profoundest outcome of our discussion. The concretely given in its eternal totality is the perfect whole. There is no heaven-by-itself, no real-in-itself. Reality is what it is found to be through all these appearances, forms, and symbols. Eternity is nothing without time, and time is nothing without eternity. Nothing is to be scorned, everything is to be included. Only we must remember that it is the perspective of the whole which reveals reality. That which is neither fair nor good alone is both good and fair in proper relation. It is when we sunder things, try to understand them by themselves, that we fall into difficulties. Separateness brings selfishness with all its attendant ills; the truth, love, beauty, is found through union. Most of our theoretical difficulties arise through abstraction; to know what the living reality is we must turn back to life. This is as true of the hermit in his cell as of the speculative metaphysician in his study, the capitalist or the labourer. Co-operation is the law of life and only through co-operation may we expect success or harmony.

Study things in immediate relation to their environment, then, if you would really know them. Study an author in the light of the age in which he lived. Do not study your own or another's virtues or vices apart from their opposites. Do not see the faults alone, but also the ideals which are being realised through them. Understand yourself as a child of your age. See how part contributes to part all through life. See mind and matter working together, man and woman, democrat and republican, nation and nation, race and race. Live in thought with the whole of the great organism, expand your being to joyful oneness with it all.

In practical life this organic philosophy is the opposite of asceticism and the condemnation of a part of life as mere appearance or evil. It points to the fitness of things, the goodness of everything in proper relations. It inspires enjoyment in nature as well as happiness in inner contemplation. One does not take less but more pleasure in being with people, more delight in all phases of life. There is a sense of freedom that the old bondage is thrown off, that one can now enjoy the present life for its own sake. Even materialism has its lesson. The materialism of the day is in a sense the delight of man in the resources of the earth. These he could not enjoy while matter was under pious condemnation. Nature may now be freely studied as a part of the great revelation of God. Man need fear nothing. There is nothing to run away from. Cowardice is now out of fashion (asceticism was cowardice). We now propose to face the whole of life, pursue it through to the end and find all there is in it, and all for the glory of God.

The chief point that I would emphasise in this chapter is the inter-relatedness of all things. I have called this relation "organic," but the figure is partly incorrect, since that would imply that the universe is one living being. All figures are inadequate to express the co-operative dependence of God, man, and nature, as a whole; and the miniature relationship corresponding to this in the soul of man. Man is more than an organ; he is a creator. Will, thought, action, art, contemplation, and the rest are more than organs in man. But the dependence is as close as that of the hand upon the eye, or the dependence of the heart on the lungs. The intimacy of relationship is the great thought. All our life contributes to each moment. Every sentiment, every perception in our minds is dependent on the divine life. We are sharers in a social life. Hundreds and thousands constantly labour for every blessing which we enjoy. No man liveth unto himself. All are indissolubly bound together. The ethical life is the natural consequence of this discovery. Our hearts should be deeply touched with gratitude that we thus share a common life, that millions serve, and that we can also serve. Each of us has a contribution to make and each in turn is a means of fuller expression of the divine ideal. Here as elsewhere, no one ideal includes all. The world exists for the glory of God, yet God exists for the world. In a sense man's life is chosen for him, yet in another sense he is free to add to the sum of ideas and accomplishments. No one conception is large enough to contain the entire truth; we must immediately qualify every statement by that which supplements it. This is the profoundest truth alike of philosophy and religion. We must worship with both the head and the heart, and also through self-denial (devotion).

All the bibles are needed, the whole of the vast visible universe, and all the inner lives of men, to express the grandeur and perfection of God. Each of us is capable of knowing and beholding all this, from his own point of view. Thus each in a sense is a trend of thought, a point of view of the divine mind. Fortunate are we if we rise to the height of this realisation, if we bear with us the knowledge that "in him we live and move and have our being." All is well if we have the right clue, if we judge the lower by the higher, if we regard the universe from the point of view of God, if we remember that each day we live we are environed by an eternal kingdom in which the Father is indissolubly related to the soul.

—

THE END

www.ingramcontent.com/pod-product-compliance
Lightning Source LLC
Chambersburg PA
CBHW081722100526
44591CB00016B/2464